MOVE IT!
STUDENTS' BOOK

SPLIT EDITION

4A

KATHERINE STANNETT AND FIONA BEDDALL

SERIES CONSULTANT: CARA NORRIS-RAMIREZ

Reading and Listening	Speaking and Pronunciation	Writing
An email	Asking for and giving information	A description of a friend
A Day in a Life Ezekiel, the Bee Guardian 🎧 Laura's career 🎧 Dictation	Expressing extremes **Pronunciation:** Compound noun word stress	Telling a story **Writing File:** Using different tenses
Making Dreams Come True It's Never Too Soon … /It's Never Too Late … 🎧 An interview with Raj 🎧 Dictation	Giving/Responding to news **Pronunciation:** Sentence stress	A biography **Writing File:** Time expressions
What's in a Smile? Does Fame Bring Happiness? 🎧 An interview with Luke, an actor 🎧 Dictation	Invitations **Pronunciation:** Showing feelings	A "for and against" essay **Writing File:** Linking words: addition and contrast
Fighting Disasters TV Saved My Life! 🎧 Talking about TV survival shows 🎧 Dictation	Asking for clarification **Pronunciation:** Consonant clusters	Giving instructions **Writing File:** Giving clear instructions

Grammar and Vocabulary

• To be and have

1 Complete the text with the correct form of *be* or *have*.

Hi. My name ¹ *is* James, and I ² .... sixteen. I ³ .... a new MP3 player. It ⁴.... red. It ⁵ .... a thousand songs on it, but it ⁶ .... (not) any rap songs because rap music ⁷ .... (not) my thing. ⁸ .... (you) an MP3 player? What ⁹ .... your favorite songs?

• Daily routines

2 Complete the phrases (1–9) with these words. Then match them to the pictures (a–i).

bus	dishes	do	~~dressed~~	make
school	take	teeth	walk	

1 get *dressed*
2 .... the dog
3 take the ....
4 .... your bed
5 do the ....
6 .... a shower
7 drive to ....
8 .... your homework
9 brush your ....

3 Which things from Exercise 2 do you do every day? What other things do you do every day?

• Present simple

4 Make sentences and questions. Use the Present simple.

1 Where / you / live / ?   *Where do you live?*
2 She / not study / geography
3 He / take a shower / every morning
4 They / drive / to the supermarket / ?
No / they. They / take / the bus
5 I / not walk / the dog / every day
6 What / she / want / for dinner?
7 He / never / watch / TV
8 She / always / do / the dishes

• Present continuous

5 Complete the phone conversation with the Present continuous form of the verbs.

A ¹ *Are you having* (you/have) a good morning?
B No, I ² .... . I ³ .... (wait) for Lucy and Grace, and I ⁴ .... (get) bored.
A Why ⁵ .... (you/wait) for them?
B My mom ⁶ .... (not/work) today, so we ⁷ .... (plan) a trip to a theme park. But Lucy and Grace ⁸ .... (travel) to my house by bus right now, and it's the slowest bus in history!

• Present simple and continuous

6 Choose the correct words.

1 I *make* / *am making* my bed at 8 o'clock every morning.
2 Where *do you go* / *are you going* now?
3 His mother is from Mexico, so she *speaks* / *is speaking* Spanish at home.
4 We never *get* / *are getting* dressed before breakfast.
5 They *stay* / *are staying* with their grandparents at the moment.
6 I *love* / *am loving* science fiction stories.
7 *Does it rain* / *Is it raining* a lot in spring?
8 He *doesn't study* / *isn't studying* French this year.

• Apostrophes

7 **Add an apostrophe to the underlined words where necessary.**

Charlie has three <u>brothers</u>. His two younger <u>brothers</u> <u>names</u> are Jack and Will, and his oldest <u>brothers</u> Fred. <u>Freds</u> an actor. He <u>isnt</u> in any famous <u>movies</u>, but he has a part in a musical called *Billy Elliot*. It <u>tells</u> the story of a boy <u>whos</u> trying to become a dancer. The <u>boys</u> dad <u>doesnt</u> want a dancer in the family, but <u>his</u> dance teacher <u>helps</u> him. <u>Its</u> a really good show.

• Pronouns and possessive adjectives

8 **Choose the correct options.**

1 Please help *me / my*.
2 *He / Him* is my best friend.
3 It isn't yours; it's *our / ours*.
4 What's *him / his* name?
5 What a big dog! Look at *it's / its* teeth.
6 Come and see *us / our* next week.
7 They want a cell phone like *mine / my*.
8 Do you like *they / them*?
9 I can't see *you / your*.

• Useful adjectives

9 **Complete the sentences with these words.**

awesome	beautiful	~~colorful~~	dirty	disgusting
huge	popular	quiet	sore	tiny

1 Her clothes are very *colorful*. She loves wearing orange and purple.
2 I live in a .... village. There are no noisy streets here.
3 Basketball is a very .... sport for boys in the US. Almost everyone plays it.
4 She's .... at math. She never gets a wrong answer!
5 My boots are .... . I must clean them.
6 This food is .... . I can't eat it.
7 Go and see the doctor about your .... throat.
8 An elephant is a .... animal.
9 A chihuahua is a .... type of dog, usually only 15 cm tall.
10 It's a .... , sunny day.

• Comparatives and superlatives

10 **Complete the sentences with these words. Use comparatives or superlatives.**

clothes	Danny Dream's	guitar	hair
Little Luke	music	Robbie T	~~singer~~

Danny Dream

Little Luke

Robbie T

1 Danny Dream is the *worst singer*. (bad)
2 Danny Dream is .... than .... . (tall)
3 Robbie T has the .... . (short)
4 Danny Dream is .... than .... . (popular)
5 Robbie T is wearing the .... . (colorful)
6 Robbie T's guitar is .... than .... guitar. (big)
7 Danny Dream has the .... . (tiny)
8 Robbie T plays the .... . (quiet)

11 **Make six sentences about people you know with the comparative or superlative of these adjectives.**

annoying	bad	cool	famous	good	thin

• Free-time activities

12 **Match 1–8 to a–h. Then match the activities to the pictures.**

1 play *d*		a	surfing
2 listen		b	gymnastics
3 use		c	text messages
4 send		d	the saxophone *picture g*
5 go		e	to rap music
6 do		f	basketball
7 play		g	a horror movie
8 watch		h	the Internet

13 **Copy and complete the table with these words.**

classical	comedy	~~drums~~	fantasy	horror
ice hockey	judo	keyboard	reggae	rock
skiing	swimming	tennis	~~track~~	violin

Sports with *do*	Sports with *go*	Sports with *play*
track	….	….

Musical instruments	Types of movies	Types of music
drums	….	….

• Relative pronouns

14 **Complete the sentences with *who*, *which* or *where*.**

1 That's the girl *who* lives next to my uncle.
2 A bank is a place …. you can get cash.
3 Which is the classroom …. Ms. Tucker teaches?
4 Is that the coat …. you're borrowing from Sam?
5 This is the hospital …. my dad works.
6 I like the sausages …. they sell at the market.
7 He's the actor …. is in that historical movie.
8 They're the kids …. I see every day on the bus.

15 **Make true sentences. Use the words in the table. Then write three more sentences with *who*, *which* or *where* and your own ideas.**

1 school	place	who	you put on the floor
2 journalist	thing	which	buys things
3 rug	person	where	you can stay
4 customer			children learn
5 hotel			goes on top of a bed
6 comforter			reports the news

1 *A school is a place where children learn.*

• *Some* and *any*

16 **Complete the sentences with *some* or *any*.**

1 Do you have *any* money?
2 There aren't …. movie theaters in my town.
3 I have …. apples. Would you like one?
4 There's …. water in the plastic bottle.
5 We don't have …. homework tonight.
6 Are there …. fish in the lake?

• *Much, many* and *a lot of*

17 **Choose the correct words.**

1 She has *much / a lot of* nice clothes.
2 How *much / many* time is there before our next class?
3 We need *much / a lot of* volunteers to help us.
4 There aren't *much / many* people here.
5 Do they have *much / many* DVDs?
6 You're making too *much / a lot of* noise.
7 How *much / many* magazines do you read?
8 We have too *much / many* problems with our computer.

Feelings adjectives

18 **Complete the words.**

1 I'm ex*cite*d about our vacation next week.
2 They're feeling pretty rel _ x _ _ about the test.
3 I'm af _ _ _ d of snakes.
4 He gets really a _ _ ry when you're rude.
5 They're b _ _ _ d of rice for dinner every day.
6 I'm so e _ b _ r _ _ _ s _ d about my terrible dancing last night!
7 She's u _ _ et about her brother's accident.
8 You're j _ _ l _ _ s of her because she's pretty.
9 I'm n _ _ v _ _ s about the game. It's really important that we win it.
10 She feels l _ _ _ ly without her friends.
11 She's p _ _ _ d of her good grade on the exam.
12 I'm t _ _ ed of baseball. Let's play a different sport.

Past simple

19 **Complete the conversation. Use the Past simple form of *be*.**

A There ¹ *were* some good shows on TV last night.
B Really? I ² .... (not) at home. I ³ .... at Meg's house.
A Why ⁴ .... (you) there?
B She ⁵ .... upset about her exams.
A What ⁶ .... the problem?
B Her grades ⁷ … (not) very good, and her parents ⁸ .... angry with her.
A ⁹ .... (she) happier after your visit?
B Yes, she ¹⁰ .... .

20 **Complete the sentences with the Past simple form of the verbs.**

1 We *watched* (watch) an action movie last night.
2 They .... (seem) very happy at Katie's house.
3 I .... (argue) with Simon yesterday.
4 They .... (travel) to the island by boat.
5 She .... (study) glaciers in geography last year.

21 **Make the sentences in Exercise 20 negative.**

1 *We didn't watch an action movie last night.*

22 **Make Past simple questions and answers.**

1 you / like / the movie?   ✗
  Did you like the movie? No, I didn't.
2 they / talk / to Katie's mom   ✓
3 you and Simon / argue / about the project?   ✓
4 they / get / to the island / by plane?   ✗
5 she / study / with Mr. Davis?   ✓

Irregular verbs

23 **Read about Connor's exciting day. Copy and complete the table with the verbs in bold.**

Infinitive	Past simple
buy	*bought*

1 In the morning he **bought** some sneakers. His friend Jake **sold** them to him.
2 Then he **ate** a banana and **drank** some juice.
3 Later he **ran** in a race and **won**.
4 After the race, the organizers **spoke** to him and **gave** him a prize.
5 He **wrote** a text message and **sent** it to all his family and friends.
6 His parents **heard** the news and **felt** proud.

Telling the time

24 **Match these times to the clocks in the pictures in Exercise 23.**

a three forty-five *4*   d five past four
b three thirty   e ten to four
c two o'clock   f eleven fifteen

25 **What did you do yesterday? At what time? Write six sentences.**

At eight fifteen I went to school.

Speaking and Listening

1 Read and listen to the conversation.
1.2 **Answer the questions.**

1 Is Holly happy or sad?
2 Why does she feel this way?

2 Copy and complete the table.

Name	Yasmin
Appearance	....
Character	....
Hobbies/Interests	....

3 Act out the conversation in groups of three.

4 Complete the questions. Match them to the answers.

1 *How* are you? *b*
2 What's she .... ?
3 Is she interested .... soccer?

a No, she isn't.
b Fine, thanks.
c She's really confident.

Fraser Hey, Holly! How are you?
Holly Fine, thanks. Better than fine, in fact. I have some really good news. My cousin Yasmin is moving to Concord soon, and she's going to go to our school!
Archie Was she the girl with long dark hair who stayed with you last summer?
Holly That's right. Look, I have a photo of her on my phone.
Fraser What's she like?
Holly She's really confident … and very talkative.
Archie I remember that. She talked and talked!
Holly Well, she has a lot of interesting things to talk about.
Fraser Is she interested in soccer?
Holly No, she isn't, but she does a lot of dancing in her free time. She loves fashion and hip hop music, too. I think you'll like her.
Archie Yes, she seemed really nice last year.

Unread Message

From   holly:)brightman@my_mail

Subject   Moving to Concord!

+ Add Attachment   x

Hi Yasmin,

I'm so excited that you're moving to Concord. We'll be neighbors!

I hope you will like it here. It's a small town, but a lot of nice people live here. My best friends, Fraser and Archie, live on my street. Archie's the boy who you met last summer. Do you remember him? He's tall like me, and he has short dark hair. He's really good fun. He's sometimes a little selfish, but I don't mind. I can be selfish, too! You didn't meet Fraser, but you'll like him. He has blond hair like me. He's shy, but he's very generous. He's smart, so you can ask him for help with your homework.

There are only 700 students at Concord High, our school, so it's smaller than your school in Philadelphia. Some of the teachers give too much homework, but everyone's really friendly. There are a lot of after-school activities, and they're a good way to make new friends. Archie and I do judo after school, and Fraser plays soccer. We're all in a drama club, too. There's also a dance club. I'll try to find out more about it for you.

I'm sending a photo of you in the clothes that you bought when we went shopping. You look so cool!

Lots of love,

Holly

SEND

Reading

5. **Read Holly's message to Yasmin. Find Fraser and Archie in the photo on page 8.**

6. **Read the message again. Copy and complete the table.**

Name	Holly	Archie	Fraser
Appearance	*tall, blond hair*	....	....
Character	....	....	....
Hobbies/ Interests	....	....	....

Writing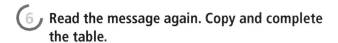

7. **Copy and complete the table about a friend of yours. Then write a paragraph about him/her.**

Name	
Appearance	
Character	
Hobbies/Interests	

My assessment profile: page 129

Different Lives

Grammar
Past simple vs
Past continuous; *used to*
for past habits

Vocabulary
Compound nouns;
Phrasal verbs 1

Speaking
Expressing extremes

Writing
Telling a story

Word list page 43
Workbook page 118

Vocabulary • Compound nouns

1 Match these words to the correct headings. Copy and complete the table.
1.3 Then listen, check and repeat.

babysitter	business person	classmate	firefighter	homework
lighthouse	skyscraper	snowmobile	spaceship	speedboat
whiteboard	windmill			

jobs	*babysitter*	....	....
transportation	....	....	....
school	....	....	....
building	....	....	....

2 Match the words in Exercise 1 to the pictures.

babysitter *10*

3 Match the clues to the correct words in Exercise 1.

1 This sends a light out across the ocean. *lighthouse*
2 This person works in an office and wears dress clothes.
3 This person stops buildings from burning down.
4 You make flour in this building.
5 A teacher uses this in class.
6 You can travel fast in this when it's very cold.
7 Some people believe that aliens travel in this.
8 You use this on the water.
9 You are probably sitting next to one now!
10 You do this after school.
11 Most big cities have these. They are very tall.
12 This person takes care of very young children.

1.4 **Pronunciation Unit 1** page 63

**Brain Trainer Unit 1
Activities 1 and 2**
Go to page 58

Reading

1 Read the article quickly. Match the people (1–3) to the photos (a–c).

2 Read the article again. Answer the questions.

1.5
1 Who was helping his/her family? *Flora and Tom*
2 Who uses a phone?
3 Who spent a long time at school?
4 Who was studying?
5 Who works in the summer?

3 In pairs, ask and answer.

1 Whose life is most like yours?
2 Which facts in the article did you find interesting/unusual/surprising?
3 Imagine you can live another person's life for one day. Whose life would you choose?

A Day in a Life

What did you do yesterday? Tell us about your life.

a

b

c

1 ....

I am a Sami Norwegian, and I live 300 kilometers north of the Arctic Circle. In the winter, I go to school with my friends in Tromsø. But in the summer, the Sami people work with reindeer, so my life is very different. Yesterday I helped my family with calf marking. We were checking our herd of reindeer and making special marks in their ears to show that they belong to our family. In the past, my family followed our herd of reindeer on wooden skis, but now we travel by snowmobile! While I was helping with the calf marking, I sent two texts to my friends in Tromsø.

Flora Turi, 15, Norway

2 ....

Yesterday was the same as every other day. I got up at 6 a.m., ate a very quick breakfast and then took the bus to school. When I got to school at seven thirty, my classmates were sweeping the classroom. I helped them, and we all sang our national anthem. Between 8 a.m. and noon, I was studying, studying, studying, and after lunch, I had more classes until 4:30 p.m. Did I go home at 4:30 p.m.? No, I didn't! I stayed at school for an extra study hall. And then I went to another school for more classes. When I finally got home, it was 10 p.m. I had some dinner, and I did my homework. For Taiwanese teenagers, life is all about studying!

Tao Chen, 16, Taiwan

3 ....

I live with my family in a beautiful part of Canada. We live "off the grid"—that means that we have no electricity in our house. We don't have the Internet and we don't have phones, but we do have a radio in case of emergencies. I don't go to school—I'm homeschooled—but I learn a lot from my off-the-grid life. Yesterday I worked with my dad. We were looking at his designs for a new windmill. In the afternoon, I did some homework. I was researching some facts for a history project with other homeschooled kids. Of course, we didn't use the Internet for our research; we used an encyclopedia and other books from the local library.

Tom Renwood, 15, Canada

Grammar • Past simple vs Past continuous

Past simple	Past continuous
I got up at 6 a.m. We didn't use the Internet for my project.	We were checking our herd of reindeer. Between 8 a.m. and noon, I was studying.

Past simple and Past continuous
When I got to school, my classmates were sweeping the classroom. While I was helping, I sent some texts to my friends in Tromsø.

Grammar reference page 110

Watch Out!

Some verbs, such as *know, understand, like, love, want, have* and *hear,* are stative verbs. They don't usually take the continuous form.
(For a full list, see page 43.)

1 **Study the grammar table. Choose the correct options to complete the rules.**

　1 We use the *Past simple / Past continuous* for completed actions in the past.
　2 We use the *Past simple / Past continuous* to describe a continuing situation in the past.
　3 We usually use the *Past simple / Past continuous* after *when,* and the *Past simple / Past continuous* after *while.*

2 **Complete the text with the correct form of the verbs.**

Hi Ted,
I ¹ *didn't have* (not have) a good day yesterday. First, I ² .... (not hear) my alarm clock, and I ³ .... (sleep) until 8 o'clock. I was late for my first class. When I ⁴ .... (go) into the classroom, the teacher ⁵ .... (talk) about the homework. My classmates ⁶ .... (take) a lot of notes, but I ⁷ .... (not have) my notebook because I ⁸ .... (leave) my schoolbag at home. So the teacher ⁹ .... (shout) at me, and he ¹⁰ .... (give) me extra homework.
What about you? ¹¹ .... (you/have) a good day yesterday?
Sam

3 **Choose the correct options.**

Last weekend my brother and I ¹ *went / were going* for a bike ride. We ² *took / were taking* a train to downtown Chicago, and then we ³ *rode / were riding* our bikes to Grant Park. While we ⁴ *rode / were riding* down the street, we ⁵ *saw / were seeing* a car crash. We ⁶ *stopped / were stopping* and ⁷ *called / were calling* an ambulance. When the ambulance ⁸ *arrived / was arriving*, the drivers ⁹ *sat / were sitting* on the pavement, and they ¹⁰ *argued / were arguing* about the accident.

4 **Make sentences.**

　1 While we / watch / TV / we / hear / a strange sound
　　While we were watching TV, we heard a strange sound.
　2 When you / call / I / do my homework
　3 I / not hear / the doorbell / because / I / listen / to my MP3 player
　4 I / see / a strange cat in the yard / while / I / wash / the car
　5 She / drop / a plate / while / she / do / the dishes

5 **What about you?** In pairs, ask and answer the questions.

　1 What did you do the day before yesterday?
　2 What were you doing between 2 p.m. and 5 p.m. last Saturday?
　3 Where did you go last weekend?
　4 What did you see on your way to school today?
　5 When did you last use your cell phone? Who were you talking to?

Vocabulary • Phrasal verbs 1

1 Read the text and complete these phrasal verbs
1.6 with the correct preposition. Then listen, check
and repeat.

1 count *on*
2 fill ....
3 find ....
4 get ....
5 give ....
6 go ....
7 hang ....
8 look ....
9 run ....
10 set ....

Word list page 43 **Workbook** page 118

I usually hang out with my friends in the summer and go
out a lot. But last year I set up a dog-walking service with
my sister. Customers could count on us to take their dogs
for a walk anytime! Our favorite pet was a dog named
Tyson. On his first walk, he ran away. We looked for him
for several hours, but finally we gave up. We went to the
police station and filled out a "missing pet" form. "What
will the owner say when he finds out?" my sister asked.
When we got back to the owner's house, we saw Tyson.
He was waiting for us at the front door!

2 Match the phrasal verbs to these definitions.

1 to rely or depend on *count on*
2 to complete a form
3 to spend time in a place doing nothing
4 to escape
5 to discover or learn new information
6 to arrange or organize
7 to stop doing something
8 to return
9 to search
10 to leave home to go to a social event

3 Match the pictures (a–e) to the conversations (1–5).
1.7 Then complete them with the correct form of the
phrasal verbs. Listen and check your answers.

1 **A** Can I ¹ *count on* you to watch your little sister
this afternoon? I have a meeting in New York.
B OK, but please don't ² .... late because I'm
³.... to Tanya's birthday party in the evening.

2 **A** What did you do yesterday? Did you ⁴ ....
with your friends in the park?
B No, I didn't. I went online and ⁵ ....
a Facebook page for my band.

3 **A** I'm trying to ⁶ .... this form online, but my
computer isn't working. I can't do it!
B Don't ⁷ .... ! Print out the form and mail it.

4 **A** My cat ⁸ .... yesterday. He got on the bus and
traveled around town.
B How did you ⁹ .... where he was?
A The bus driver saw the tag on his collar and
called me.

5 **A** Are you ¹⁰ .... something?
B Yes, I am. I can't find my favorite T-shirt!

4 Work in pairs. Choose at least four phrasal verbs
from Exercise 1 and write a short conversation.

Brain Trainer Unit 1
Activity 3
Go to page 58

Speaking and Listening

1 Look at the photo. Can you remember how the girls know each other?

2 Listen and read the conversation.
1.8 Check your answer.

3 Listen and read again. Answer the questions.
1.8
  1 Why is Yasmin in Concord?
    She lives there now.
  2 What does she think of it?
  3 What does Archie think of the town?
  4 What does Yasmin's mom do?
  5 Does Yasmin's house have an amazing yard?

4 Act out the conversation in groups of four.

Holly	Hi, Fraser! Hi, Archie! This is my cousin, Yasmin.
Archie	Hey, Yasmin. We met last summer, remember?
Yasmin	Yes, of course. And now I live here! I love Concord. It's such a cool town!
Archie	Cool! I don't think so. It's really boring. It's so small, and there's nothing to do in the evening.
Yasmin	Well, I used to live in a really busy city, and I hated it. It was so noisy.
Fraser	Why did your family move here?
Yasmin	My mom wanted to get out of the city. She used to have such a stressful job, but she gave it up and set up her own business as a landscape designer.
Fraser	So do you live in a house with an amazing yard now?
Yasmin	Yeah, right! It's a junkyard. But Mom has a lot of plans.

Say it in your language …
I don't think so!
Yeah, right!

5 Find and complete these sentences with *so* or *such*. Which word comes before an adjective without a noun?

1 It's *such* a cool town!
2 It's …. small, and there's nothing to do in the evening.
3 It was …. noisy.
4 She used to have …. a stressful job.

6 Read the phrases for expressing extremes.

Expressing extremes	
so	It was **so** noisy. The skyscrapers are **so** tall. I'm **so** hungry.
such	It's **such** a cool town! He's **such** a nice man. It's **such** a hot day today.
really	It's **really** boring. I used to live in a **really** busy city.

7 Listen to the conversations. Act out the conversations in pairs.
1.9

Holly I love this ¹ movie. It's so ² funny!
Yasmin I agree. And ³ Amy Poehler is such a ⁴ great actor.

Archie You have such a ⁵ big house, Fraser.
Fraser It is ⁶ big, but ⁷ it's so chilly in the winter.

8 Work in pairs. Replace the words in purple in Exercise 7. Use these words and/or your own ideas. Act out the conversations.

1 band / book

2 talented / exciting

3 Adam Levine / the author

4 good singer / wonderful writer

5 nice room / small phone

6 beautiful / small

7 hot in summer / difficult to use

Grammar • Used to

Affirmative		
I/He/She/We/You/They	used to	live in a big city.
Negative		
I/He/She/We/You/They	didn't use to	have a car.

Questions and short answers	
Did I/he/she/we/you/they use to read comics when I/he/she/we/you/they was/were younger?	Yes, I/he/she/we/you/they did.
	No, I/he/she/we/you/they didn't.

Wh questions
Who used to teach English at this school?

Grammar reference page 110

1 Study the grammar table. Complete the rules with *used to* or *use to* and choose the correct options.

1 We use …. to talk about *habits / completed actions* in the past.
2 We form the positive with …. + infinitive.
3 We form the negative with *didn't* and …. + infinitive.
4 We form questions with *Did* + subject + …. + infinitive.

2 Complete the sentences with the correct form of *used to* and the verbs in parentheses.

1 My sister *used to love* (love) chocolate, but now she hates it.
2 I …. (not walk) to school, but now I walk there every day.
3 Where did you …. (go) on vacation?
4 **A** …. (you be) on the basketball team?
   B Yes, I did. But I …. (not enjoy) it.
5 We …. (not spend) much time in the park.
6 What …. (you do) after school when you lived in Detroit?

3 Complete these sentences with your own ideas.

1 When I was five, I didn't use to …
2 I always used to like … , but now …
3 My family used to … , but now …

Reading

1 Read the article quickly. Which sentence is the best summary of the article?

1 Ezekiel Barzey started The Golden Company because he was scared of bees.
2 Ezekiel Barzey's experience of beekeeping changed his life.
3 Ezekiel Barzey used to work for a bank, but now he makes honey.

Ezekiel, the Bee Guardian

"I used to be a completely different person," says Ezekiel Barzey, age 19. "I used to hang out with my friends, and we got into trouble with the police. I felt excluded, and I only saw the negative things in my community." But when Ezekiel was 17 years old, he got involved in a project run by Zoe Palmer, and his life began to change.

Zoe used to be a moviemaker for a TV nature channel, and she spent some time in Albania, filming bees and beekeepers. She was impressed by the relaxed and calm atmosphere around the beekeepers. When she got back to Britain, she set up The Golden Company. It teaches young people in London about beekeeping and gives them the opportunity to connect with nature and to find out how to develop, market and sell honey products.

Ezekiel is now a "Bee Guardian," and he takes care of a hive on the roof garden of the Nomura Investment Bank, in the heart of the City of London. The bank buys all the honey and uses it at meetings and business breakfasts. There are several other hives in London, and they all have special Bee Guardians from The Golden Company. Ezekiel also helps to run a stand at a local market in the city. He and other Bee Guardians make beauty products from honey and sell them at the stand.

Ezekiel was scared of the bees when he started his training, but he learned to calm down and not to panic. Now the bees can count on him to take care of them. "I'm more in touch with nature now," he explains. "I understand how bees operate!" He is also much more confident about himself and his role in society. "Now I have a chance in life to become successful," he says. "I'm glad the company was there for me when I needed it."

Key Words

excluded	get involved
beekeeping/beekeeper	honey
hive	stand

2 Read the article again. Answer the questions.

1.10

1 Why did Ezekiel's life change when he was 17 years old?
Because he got involved in a project run by Zoe Palmer.
2 What impressed Zoe Palmer in Albania?
3 What is The Golden Company?
4 Where is the hive that Ezekiel takes care of?
5 How does the bank use the honey?
6 What do Ezekiel and the other Bee Guardians make from the honey?
7 How did Ezekiel's feelings about bees change?
8 How did Ezekiel's feelings about himself change?

Listening

1 Listen to the radio show and choose the correct summary.

1.11

1 Laura taught the trumpet, and changed someone's life.
2 Laura heard the trumpet, and it changed her life.
3 Laura found a trumpet on the street, and it changed her life.

 Listening Bank Unit 1 page 61

2 Think about a famous person, for example, a sports star, a musician or an actor, and imagine how that person chose his/her career.

1 What important moment do you imagine changed his/her life? Why was it important?
2 Was there an important moment in your life that changed you? How? What happened?

Writing • Telling a story

1 Read the Writing File.

> **Writing File** Using different tenses
>
> **We often use a mix of tenses when we tell a story in the past.**
>
> - **We use the Past simple to describe a series of events.**
>   I jumped out of bed, got dressed and went down to the kitchen.
> - **We use the Past continuous for descriptions and continuous actions.**
>   It was raining and a dog was barking.
> - **We use the Present simple in dialogues and to describe states and things that don't change.**
>   "I don't feel well today," she said.
>   My family lives in a small house near the ocean.

2 Make sentences. Choose the correct tense from Exercise 1.

1 Last weekend / I / visit / my aunt / and then / I / go / to the movies
Last weekend I visited my aunt, and then I went to the movies.

2 I / usually / get up / at 7 o'clock

3 Yesterday afternoon / my sister / read / a magazine / when / the doorbell / ring

4 "you / like / chocolate?" asked my teacher

3 Read the story on the right. Find these tenses.

- Present simple
- Past simple
- Present continuous
- Past continuous

4 Read the story again. Answer the questions.

1 What did Gina do after she got up?
She had breakfast and helped her dad in the yard.

2 Was the weather good or bad?

3 Why was Gina not happy?

4 What is Gina always doing?

5 What prize did Gina win?

6 Where does Gina's family usually go on vacation?

An Amazing Day by Gina Bett

Yesterday was an amazing day. It began as usual— a typical boring Saturday. I got up, had breakfast and helped my dad in the yard. The sun was shining, and the birds were singing in the sky, but I was in a bad mood because I had a lot of homework, and I wanted to go out with my friends. Then my mom came outside. She was holding a letter.

"It's for you!" she said.

I read the letter quickly and shouted, "I don't believe it!"

"What is it?" asked my mom.

"I entered a contest last week," I replied, "Do you remember?"

Well, of course she didn't remember. I'm always entering contests, and I never win anything. But this time it was different.

"I won first prize," I said. "A family vacation in Florida!"

We all shouted and laughed. Then we ran inside and started to plan our vacation. We usually go camping in the rain—but not this year!

5 You are going to write a short story with the title *An Unusual Day.* Plan your story. Think about these things.

- Who are the main characters in the story?
- What happens to them?
- How do they feel?
- What happens at the end of the story?

6 Now write your story. Use your ideas from Exercise 5.

> **Remember!**
> - Use a mix of tenses.
> - Use the vocabulary in this unit.
> - Check your grammar, spelling and punctuation.

Refresh Your Memory!

Grammar • Review

1 Match the sentence beginnings (1–5) to the endings (a–e).

1 The sun was shining brightly, *b*
2 When I got to the bus stop,
3 I sat down
4 I was waiting for the bus
5 While I was running toward the child,

a I dropped my bag.
b and the birds were singing.
c and waited for the next bus.
d the bus was already disappearing down the street.
e when I saw a child in the middle of the street.

2 Complete the text with the correct form of the verbs, Past simple or Past continuous.

I ¹ *was eating* (eat) my lunch when the phone
² .... (ring). I ³ .... (stand) up quickly and ⁴ .... (run)
toward the phone. While I ⁵ .... (run), I ⁶ .... (trip)
over the dog and ⁷ .... (hurt) my leg. I ⁸ .... (try)
to stand up again when I ⁹ .... (hear) the doorbell.
I ¹⁰ .... (walk) slowly to the door and ¹¹ .... (open)
it. It was my friend, Kate. "Are you OK?" she
asked. "You ¹² .... (not/answer) the phone."

3 Make sentences with *used to* and *didn't use to* and the information in the chart.

When John was five …

play soccer	✗
be scared of the dark	✓
believe in ghosts	✓
have a lot of homework	✗
ride a bike to school	✗
like chocolate	✓
climb trees in the park	✓

When John was five, he didn't use to play soccer.

Vocabulary • Review

4 Match the words in box *a* to the words in box *b* to make compound nouns.

a	baby*sitter*	business	class	fire
	home	light	sky	snow
	space	speed	white	wind

b	board	boat	fighter	house
	mate	mill	mobile	person
	scraper	ship	~~sitter~~	work

5 Complete the sentences with the correct form of these phrasal verbs.

count on	fill out	get back	give up
go out	hang out	look for	~~set up~~

1 My mother *set up* her own travel company when she was 20 years old.
2 I know that the homework is difficult, but don't .... !
3 Please .... this form to apply for the job.
4 I .... my jacket in my bedroom, but I couldn't find it.
5 Last night we .... to a few clubs downtown.
6 When you need help, you can always .... me.
7 I usually .... with my friends on the weekend.
8 I usually .... from school at 4 o'clock.

Speaking • Review

6 Complete the conversation with the correct words.
1.12 Then listen and check.

A I don't like this town. It's ¹ *so / such* boring!
B I don't agree. I think it's ² *such / really* great.
It has ³ *such / really* a fantastic park, and the gym is ⁴ *so / such* cheap.
A Well, that's true. But we live ⁵ *so / such* a long way from the center of town. And the buses are ⁶ *so / such* expensive.
B True, but you have a ⁷ *so / really* big house with a nice yard. You're ⁸ *so / such* lucky!

Dictation

7 Listen and write in your notebook.
1.13

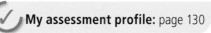
✓ My assessment profile: page 130

Biology File

Where Are All the Bees?

1 .C. All around the world, reports warn that bees are flying away from their hives and not returning. Farmers, scientists and environmental groups are worried, and they are trying to find out why it's happening.

2 .... Are they so important to our environment? The short answer is yes, it does matter, and yes, they are important. Bees fly around from flower to flower, looking for nectar and pollen. They use these to produce honey, which is food for their colonies. But at the same time, the bees help to move pollen from one flower to another. This process is called "pollination." Pollination means that the flowers can create seeds and new flowers. Without bees, many flowers can't make seeds or fruit. In fact, bees are responsible for the pollination of one-third of all of the plants that we eat. A single hive with 50,000 honeybees can pollinate 500,000 plants in one day! Imagine a world with no apples, carrots, onions, raspberries, strawberries or, of course, honey. That's a world with no bees.

3 .... Scientists think that there are several possible reasons, including climate change, disease and pesticides (chemicals that kill insects).

4 .... Beekeeping was popular two or three hundred years ago, when many families kept their own hives for honey. Now beekeeping is becoming popular again in towns and cities, as well as in the country. In fact, towns are actually good places for hives because they have gardens and parks with a lot of different types of flowers. Elementary schools, businesses, universities and community centers are now setting up their own hives. They enjoy the delicious honey, and at the same time they know that they are helping to take care of some of the most important insects on the planet.

Reading

1 **Read the article quickly. Match these sentences to the correct paragraphs.**

  a But it's not all bad news.
  b But does it really matter if bees disappear?
  c Bees are disappearing.
  d So, why are the bees disappearing?

2 **Read the article again. Answer the questions.**

1.14
  1 Why are farmers, scientists and environmental groups worried about bees?
  2 Why do bees fly from one flower to another?
  3 What is pollination?
  4 How many plants can one bee pollinate in one day?
  5 What possible causes are there for the bees' disappearance?
  6 Why are towns good environments for beekeeping?

3 **Listen to some more information on bees. Choose**
1.15 **the correct numbers to complete the fact file.**

  | 6.5 6 4,000 one-twelfth (¹/₁₂) ~~25,000~~ 24 |

Bee Fact File Did you know …?

- There are around [1] 25,000 species of bees in the world.
- There are over [2] .... species of bees in the US.
- A bee produces [3] .... of a teaspoon of honey in its life.
- The average life of a worker bee is [4] .... weeks.
- Bees fly [5] .... kilometers on an average trip.
- They can fly [6] .... kilometers per hour.

My Biology File

4 **You are going to produce a pamphlet about butterflies. Find out the following information about them.**

- How they find food
- Why they are important for the environment
- If they face the same problems as bees
- How we can protect them
- How many species there are in the world/in your country

5 **Work in pairs and make your pamphlet. Include pictures or photos if possible.**

Aiming High

Grammar
Present perfect; Present
perfect vs Past simple

Vocabulary
Collocations with *make*,
go and *keep*; Jobs and
suffixes

Speaking
Giving/Responding to news

Writing
A biography

Word list page 43
Workbook page 119

Vocabulary • Collocations with *make*, *go* and *keep*

1 Copy the table. Put these phrases under the correct verbs. Then listen, check and repeat. 1.16

a decision
a difference
a secret
calm
control
crazy
for a walk
in touch
it to the finals
together
someone's dream
come true
well

make	keep	go
a decision	....	....

2 Match the phrases from Exercise 1 to the definitions.

1 not tell someone about something *keep a secret*
2 become very excited about something or be very impractical
3 combine well with something
4 succeed in a sport so that you will play in the most important game
5 have an important effect on something
6 communicate with someone
7 choose to do something
8 achieve an ambition or a hope
9 make a short journey on foot
10 manage
11 don't get angry or upset
12 happen in a good way

3 Complete the cartoons with the correct form of a collocation from Exercise 1. Then listen and check your answers. 1.17

1.18 **Pronunciation Unit 2** page 63

1 Hannah goes *crazy* every time she hears One Direction.

2 This morning is not going ....! I can't find my favorite One Direction CD.

3 It's a surprise present for your sister. Can you keep ....?

4 I can't believe it! You made ....!

**Brain Trainer Unit 2
Activities 1 and 2**
Go to pages 58–59

Reading

1. Look at the large photo. In pairs, discuss. Why is this soccer field unusual? Where do you think it is?

2. Read the article quickly and put the events (a–e) in the correct order.

   a Panyee SC won the Youth Soccer Tournament.
   b The boys built a soccer field.
   c The boys were watching the World Cup on TV. *1*
   d Panyee SC got to the semifinals of a local soccer tournament.
   e The boys practiced their soccer skills on the wooden field.

3. Read the article again. Answer the questions.
   1.19
   1 What is the main industry of Koh Panyee? *fishing*
   2 How many families live on Koh Panyee?
   3 What inspired the boys to form a soccer team?
   4 Why did the villagers laugh at the boys?
   5 What materials did the boys use to make the soccer field?
   6 How did the boys become so good at soccer?

4. What about you? In pairs, ask and answer.
   • What sports facilities do you have in your town or city?
   • Can you think of ways to improve them?
   • Do you know of any other unusual places where people play sports?

Making Dreams Come True

In a small fishing village in southern Thailand, some boys enthusiastically play soccer. They run, shout, jump and kick like most other soccer players, but these boys are especially good at keeping control of the ball. Why? Because their soccer field is a raft in the middle of the ocean! They live on the island of Koh Panyee, where all the houses are on stilts. The island has a total population of three hundred families, but although the village is small, its success on the soccer field has been huge. Since 2004, the Panyee Soccer Club has won the Thai Youth Soccer Tournament seven times.

The story of Panyee SC begins back in 1986. Some of the young boys from the village were watching the World Cup Soccer Tournament on television. Suddenly, one of the boys said, "We watch soccer on TV, but we've never played it." The boys made a decision. "Our soccer team starts today. We want to become world champions!" they shouted. But the villagers laughed at them. "Are you crazy? Have you ever played soccer?" they asked. "You've already formed a team, but you haven't found a field yet! How can you practice?"

The boys were determined to make their dream come true. They used old fishing boats and pieces of wood to make a floating soccer field. They practiced for hours every day, even when the field was wet, and developed amazing skills. That first year, they made it to the semifinals of the local soccer tournament. Panyee SC has now played for over twenty-five years and is one of the best youth soccer teams in the country.

Grammar • Present perfect

Present perfect + *ever, never, already, yet*

The village's success on the soccer field has been huge.

Have you ever played soccer?

We watch soccer on TV, but we have never played it.

You've already formed a soccer team, but you haven't found a field yet!

Grammar reference page 112

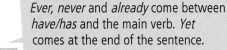

Watch Out!
Ever, never and *already* come between *have/has* and the main verb. *Yet* comes at the end of the sentence.

I've never been to a soccer game.
The team hasn't scored a goal yet.

1 Study the grammar table and Watch Out! Complete the rules with these words.

already	ever	never	yet

1 We use .... with questions. It means "at any time."
2 .... means "at no time."
3 .... means "earlier than expected."
4 (not) .... means that something we expected to happen has not happened at that point.

2 Make questions with *ever.* Answer the questions.

1 you / play / beach volleyball?
Have you ever played beach volleyball?
Yes, I have./No, I haven't.
2 you / sleep / on a train?
3 your family / travel / to Africa?
4 you / swim / in the ocean?
5 you / meet / a famous actor?

3 Choose the correct options.

Joe Didn't you need to call your aunt, Tom?
Tom I've ¹ *already / ever* talked to her. And guess what? She gave my brother and me tickets to watch the Chicago Cubs at Wrigley Field!
Joe Wow! I've ² *never / ever* been to Wrigley Field. You're so lucky.
Tom I know! I haven't told my brother ³ *ever / yet*. He's ⁴ *yet / already* gone to bed because he doesn't feel well.
Joe Have you ⁵ *already / ever* been to a Cubs game before?
Tom Yes, I saw them play last year. It was amazing!

Present perfect with *since* and *for*

Since 2004, the Panyee Soccer Club has won the Thai Youth Soccer Tournament seven times.

Panyee SC has now played for over twenty-five years.

4 Read the grammar table and choose the correct options.

1 We use the Present perfect with *for / since* to talk about a period of time.
2 We use the Present perfect with *for / since* to talk about something that started at a point in time in the past.

5 Copy the table and put these time words/phrases in the correct column.

ever	a few minutes	~~two weeks~~
last summer	the last time I saw you	~~my birthday~~
several years	she was a child	two hours
2010		

for	since
two weeks	*my birthday*

6 What about you? **In pairs, ask and answer.**

1 What have you already done today?
2 What important things have you not done yet this week?
3 How many text messages have you sent since yesterday?
4 What have you never done, but want to do?

Vocabulary • Jobs and suffixes
-or, -er, -ist

1 Match these words to the items in the picture
1.20 (1–12). Then listen, check and repeat.

art	artist	novel	novelist
photograph	photographer	play	playwright
poem	poet	sculptor	sculpture *1*

Word list page 43
Workbook page 119

2 Match the pairs of words from Exercise 1.

art	*artist*
novel	....
photograph	....
play	....
poem	....
sculpture	....

3 Use the suffixes *-or*, *-er* or *-ist* to make more jobs.
In your notebook, draw wordwebs like this one
to record your words.

.... ← **-or** → doctor
↓
....

4 Work in pairs. Choose a job from Exercise 1 or 3.
Say three words related to the job, but don't use
the word itself. Can your partner guess the job?

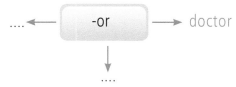

house, bricks, roof

Builder!

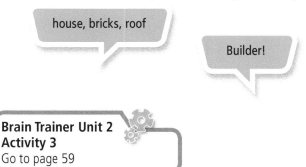

**Brain Trainer Unit 2
Activity 3**
Go to page 59

Speaking and Listening

1. **Look at the photo. Who has been playing Frisbee?**

2. **Listen and read the conversation.**
   1.21 **Check your answer.**

3. **Listen and read again. Answer the questions.**
   1.21
   1. Who is probably worse at playing Frisbee than Yasmin? *Archie*
   2. Who is Mr. Turnbull?
   3. What has Mr. Turnbull just won?
   4. Does Holly think that Mr. Turnbull is a good singer?
   5. Why is Fraser surprised about the chocolate bar advertisement?

4. **Act out the conversation in groups of four.**

Yasmin	I dropped it again. I'm a lost cause!
Holly	You've never played with Archie! He can't catch to save his life!
Fraser	Shh! Look, he's over there. He's waving at us. You're late, Archie. What's up?
Archie	You'll never believe this!
Holly	What?
Archie	I just heard some amazing news.
Yasmin	Yeah? Come on, what happened?
Archie	Well, I was reading the paper, and you won't believe it, but Mr. Turnbull, the soccer coach, has won a national songwriting contest.
Yasmin	No way!
Holly	Mr. Turnbull, a songwriter? You're kidding me! He looks like he can't even sing in tune.
Archie	Seriously. I swear it's true. He wrote the music for a chocolate bar advertisement on TV last year.
Fraser	Unbelievable! And he's always saying that chocolate is bad for us!

Say it in your language ...

I'm a lost cause!

He can't catch to save his life!

5 **Look back at the conversation. Find these expressions.**

1 Two ways to say: *Tell me about it.*
What's up?

2 Three ways to say: *I don't believe you!*

3 One way to say: *It's true.*

6 **Read the phrases for giving and responding to news.**

Giving news
I just heard some amazing news.
You won't believe it, but …

Asking about news
What's up?
What happened?

Responding to news
No way!
You're kidding me!
Unbelievable!

Confiming news
Seriously.
I swear it's true.

7 **Listen to the conversations. Act out**
1.22 **the conversations in pairs.**

Yasmin I just heard some amazing news!
Fraser What happened?
Yasmin ¹ My uncle just got a job as principal of our school.
Fraser No way!

Holly You won't believe it, but ² I won first prize in a poetry contest.
Archie You're kidding me!
Holly Seriously.

Yasmin What's up, Fraser?
Fraser ³ I just found twenty bucks in my pocket.
Yasmin Unbelievable!

8 **Work in pairs and practice the conversations in Exercise 7. Replace the words in purple. Use these phrases and/or your own ideas.**

1 my brother / get into drama school

2 my dog / win / first prize in a pet show

3 my dad / buy a Porsche

Grammar • Present perfect vs Past simple

Present perfect
Mr. Turnbull has won a songwriting contest.

Past simple
He wrote the music for a chocolate bar advertisement on TV last year.

Grammar reference page 112

1 **Study the grammar table. Choose the correct options to complete the rules.**

1 We use the *Past simple / Present perfect* to talk about an action at an unspecified time in the past or in an unfinished time period that has a result in the present.

2 We use the *Past simple / Present perfect* to talk about an action at a specified time in the past.

2 **Complete the sentences. Use the Present perfect or Past simple form of the verbs.**

1 Yesterday I *got up* (get up) early and *went* (go) for a run before breakfast.

2 We …. (not see) Mark since last Christmas.

3 They …. (not watch) a DVD yesterday; they …. (listen) to some music.

4 …. (you/see) the new Batman movie? It's awesome!

3 **Complete the news report with the correct form of these verbs.**

break	join	never win
take part in	teach	~~win~~

Schoolteacher Is Swimming Star!

Math teacher Sarah Lee ¹ *has won* an international swim meet. Ms. Lee ² …. Fairbridge School two months ago, but she also works at Goldfins Swimming Club, where she ³ …. swimming for several years. On January 22 she ⁴ …. the 800 meters freestyle swimming record. "I ⁵ …. in hundreds of swim meets since I was a child," said Ms. Lee, "but I ⁶ …. a medal before!"

4 **Work in pairs. Imagine you have achieved something amazing! Interview each other. Use the Present perfect and Past simple.**

It's Never Too Soon ... to Aim for Success

Nancy Yi Fan was just 11 years old in 2004 when she started to write *Swordbird*—a fantasy novel about birds. She spent two years writing it, and then emailed the book to several large publishing companies in the US. Just one month later, in 2006, Nancy had a publishing deal and became one of the youngest published novelists in the US. But what makes Nancy's achievement even more impressive is the fact that English isn't her first language. Nancy was born to Chinese parents in China, and the family moved to the US when she was seven years old. In 2008 *Swordbird* reached the top of the *New York Times* bestseller list. Nancy has now written a prequel to *Swordbird*, called *Sword Quest,* and she's also translated *Swordbird* into Chinese!

It's Never Too Late ... to Learn Something New

In 1989 a gallery in Sydney, Australia, presented an exhibition of Aboriginal art. The exhibition was a huge success, and many art dealers and gallery owners became particularly interested in one of the artists there—Emily Kngwarreye. This artist's painting, *Emu Woman*, was the image on the front cover of the exhibition catalogue. The art world of Australia wanted to know more about this extraordinary artist. "Who is she?" they wondered. "What else has she already painted?" Amazingly, Kngwarreye was a 79-year-old Aboriginal woman, and *Emu Woman* was her first ever painting on canvas. In the following eight years, Kngwarreye produced nearly 3,000 paintings (approximately one painting per day). She died in 1999, and is now one of Australia's most famous abstract artists. Her paintings have become famous around the world. Not a bad achievement for an artist who only began painting at the age of 78!

Key Words

publishing deal	impressive
bestseller	art dealer
gallery owner	canvas

Reading

1 **Read the article quickly. Choose the correct option.**

  1 Nancy/Emily became famous at the age of 79.
  2 Nancy/Emily has written two books.
  3 Nancy/Emily is alive today.
  4 Nancy/Emily produced thousands of paintings.

2 **Read the article again. Find the important events**
1.23 **for these dates.**

  1 1989
    There was an exhibition of Aboriginal art in Sydney, Australia.
  2 1999
  3 2004
  4 2006
  5 2008

Listening

1 **Listen to the news show and match the people (1–4)**
1.24 **to the descriptions (a–d).**

  1 Raj Patel   a US talk show host
  2 Nisha Patel   b musician
  3 Jennifer Marquez   c student
  4 Larry Nixon   d actor

 Listening Bank Unit 2 page 61

2 **In pairs, ask and answer.**

  1 Do you like listening to rap music?
  2 Have you ever tried to write a rap song?
  3 What kind of music videos do you like to watch?
  4 Have you ever uploaded a video online? What did the video present?

Writing • A biography

1 **Read the Writing File.**

> **Writing File** Time expressions
>
> **When you write about a person's life, you can use different expressions of time.**
>
> - **… years/months ago**
>   Twenty-five years ago, Henry lived in a small house in the country.
>
> - **during + period of time**
>   During his childhood, he became interested in poetry.
>
> - **when + pronoun + was**
>   When Henry was 12 years old, he won a national poetry contest.
>
> - **in + year/month**
>   In 2006 he decided to move to Nigeria.
>
> - **the following year/month**
>   The following year, he met Jodie Taylor.
>
> - **period of time + later**
>   Two years later, they got married.
>
> - **after + period of time**
>   After several months, they set up an online business.

2 **Complete the sentences with the correct time word from the box.**

> after   during   following   ~~in~~   when

1 My aunt was born *in* 1967.
2 …. she was 17 years old, she left school and traveled to India.
3 …. her stay in India, she worked for the "Save the Children" charity.
4 …. three years in India, she decided to return to the US and set up her own charity.
5 The …. year, she organized a charity fashion show in New York.

3 **Read the biography and find the time expressions.**

Katy Perry was born as Katheryn Elizabeth Hudson in *1984* in Santa Barbara, California. Her parents worked as Christian pastors, and her family wasn't very musical. But Katy often sang in her parents' church during her childhood.

When Katy was 17 years old, she moved to Los Angeles to start a career in music. It was a difficult time for her. She lived on her own, and she worked hard to get a deal in a record company, but she wasn't successful.

Five years later, in 2007, the recording company Capitol offered her a contract. In 2008 Katy's first album, *One of the Boys*, came out, and it was a huge success.

Katy released her second album, *Teenage Dream*, in 2010. Three years later, her third album, *Prism*, came out. Katy Perry is a true star now, and she has won many awards for her amazing, fun music.

4 **Read the biography again and complete the timeline.**

1984	Katy Perry was born.
2001	She moved to Los Angeles.
	The recording company Capitol offered her a contract.
2008	
2010	
	She released her third album, *Prism*.

5 **Make a timeline like the one in Exercise 4. Make it about a family member or a famous person.**

6 **Write a biography. Use your timeline in Exercise 5 and the sample biography in Exercise 3 to help you.**

> **Remember!**
> - Use expressions of time.
> - Use the vocabulary in this unit.
> - Check your grammar, spelling and punctuation.

Refresh Your Memory!

Grammar • Review

1 **Complete the sentences with *already, ever, never* or *yet*.**

1 **A** Have you *ever* met a famous actor?
  B No, I haven't.
2 **A** Why aren't you laughing?
  B Because I've .... heard that joke.
3 **A** Have you read that magazine .... ?
  B Yes, I have.
4 **A** Have you started your history homework ....?
  B Yes, I've .... finished it. I did it yesterday.
5 **A** Have you guys been to the new pool .... ?
  B No. My brother has .... been swimming. He's scared of the water.

2 **Choose the correct options.**

1 My family has lived in this town *for / since* 2008.
2 I haven't seen him *for / since* last Christmas.
3 James stayed with us *for / since* two weeks over the summer.
4 She's been crazy about music *for / since* she was three years old.
5 The girls played tennis yesterday *for / since* two hours.

3 **Complete the email with the correct form of the verbs.**

> **Unread Message**
>
> Hi Sarah,
> How are you?
> ¹ *Have you met* (you/meet) my friend Sophie? She lives next to my school.
> She ² .... (just/hear) some amazing news—she ³ .... (get) into the Lincoln Arts School!
> She ⁴ .... (go) to the school for an audition last month. She ⁵ .... (sing) a song and ⁶ .... (play) the violin. She was so nervous!
> She ⁷ .... (not hear) anything from them for two weeks, but then yesterday she ⁸ .... (get) a letter from the school with an offer of admission. I'm so jealous!
> Kate xx
>
> **REPLY**

Vocabulary • Review

4 **Complete the sentences with these words.**

a decision	a difference	calm	control
~~crazy~~	for a walk	in touch	it to the finals
together	well		

1 Why are you riding your bike in the house? Have you gone *crazy*?
2 Is my outfit OK? Do you think brown and black go .... ?
3 What's the plan for this afternoon? We need to make .... soon.
4 We were so excited when our team made .... of the talent contest.
5 It's a beautiful day. Let's go .... in the park.
6 Please keep .... of your dog. He's in my yard!
7 Everyone looks bored. The party isn't going .....
8 Ted lives in Italy, but he keeps .... by email.
9 A little kindness makes .... to other people.
10 Try to keep .... and don't panic!

5 **Make jobs from these words.**

| art *artist* | novel | photograph |
| play | poem | sculpture |

Speaking • Review

6 **Complete the conversation with these words. Then listen and check.**
1.25

| ~~I just heard~~ | it's true | No way! |
| Seriously | What happened? | |

A ¹ *I just heard* some amazing news.
B Really? ² ....
A My sister has won a car!
B ³ ....
A ⁴ .... . I swear ⁵.... .
B That's incredible!

Dictation

7 **Listen and write in your notebook.**
1.26

 My assessment profile: page 131

Bruce Baillie Hamilton's Profile

Age	Home country
14 years old	Scotland

My favorite things…

languages, traveling, talking to people

The Polyglot

Bruce Baillie Hamilton, from Callander, Scotland, is only fourteen years old, but he's already a talented polyglot. Who or what is a polyglot? It's not an illness, or a strange animal; it's a term for someone who can speak several languages fluently. Bruce has recently won a contest to find "The Most Multilingual Child in the UK."

His first foreign languages were French and German, which he started learning at school when he was seven years old. At the age of nine, he decided to learn a language with a different alphabet and began to study Russian. It wasn't easy—"Russian grammar is really difficult," says Bruce—but he didn't stop. The next language was Chinese. "Chinese is interesting, even though it has no alphabet," says Bruce. "I found it hard at the beginning, but it gets easier. Now I think Chinese is the easiest of the languages to speak. When you are in China, and you can speak Chinese, the people are much friendlier."

He can also speak Spanish, Arabic and, of course, English, and he is planning to learn Lebanese Arabic soon.

Bruce is clearly a very talented and intelligent teenager, but he has also worked hard in order to learn these languages. Since the age of twelve, Bruce has spent about twenty hours a week of his free time on his language studies during the school year, and many more hours over summer breaks.

Bruce isn't the only talented linguist in his family. His brother, Angus, and his sister, Lucy, are both studying several foreign languages. It's a big surprise to his parents. "My husband and I are both awful at languages!" says his mother, Paula. "I am absolutely thrilled for Bruce. He's worked so hard, and he enjoys using the languages and communicating with them."

Reading

1. **Read Bruce's profile and look at the title of the article. What is a polyglot? Guess. Then read the article quickly to check.**

   a a person who has traveled a lot
   b a computer program to teach languages
   c a person who can speak many languages
   d a talkative person

2. **Read the article again. Answer the questions.**
   1.27

   1 How old was Bruce when he began to study French?
   2 Why did he want to learn Russian?
   3 What is unusual about the Chinese language?
   4 What does Bruce say about the people in China?
   5 Which language will Bruce learn next?
   6 How much time does Bruce spend studying languages?
   7 Why is Paula surprised that her children are good at languages?

Class discussion

1 Who can speak the most languages in your class?
2 What are the most commonly spoken languages in your country?
3 Which languages do you think are the most useful to learn? Why?

3 Be Happy!

Vocabulary • Showing feelings

1 Match the pictures (1–6) to six words in the box.

blush
cry
frown *1*
gasp
laugh
scream
shiver
shout
sigh *7*
smile
sweat
yawn

2 Listen and match the speakers (7–12) to the other
1.28 six words in the box in Exercise 1.

3 Complete the sentences with these words.

gasp	~~shout~~	sigh	sweat

1 We *shout* when we're angry.
2 We .... when we're very surprised.
3 We .... when we're hot.
4 We .... when we're fed up.

blush	frown	scream	smile

5 We .... when we're frightened.
6 We .... when we're embarrassed.
7 We .... when we're in a bad mood.
8 We .... when we're happy.

cry	laugh	shiver	yawn

9 We .... when we're cold.
10 We .... when we're tired.
11 We .... when we're upset.
12 We .... when we're amused.

4 When do you and your family do the things
in Exercise 1?
I often shiver when I get out of the swimming pool.
My mom sighs when she sees my messy room.

**Brain Trainer Unit 3
Activities 1 and 2**
Go to page 59

1.29 **Pronunciation Unit 3** page 63

Reading

1 **Read the text quickly. Is it …**

   1 an advertisement?   2 an article?   3 a review?

2 **Read the text again and answer the questions.**

1.30 1 Which language can you use all around the world?

    You can use your smile all around the world.

   2 Look at the pictures. Which picture do you think shows someone who
- is not really happy?
- is proud of something?
- is amused?

   3 What can people in a bad mood do to feel better? Find five ideas in the text.

   4 What are endorphins?

   5 According to the text, why do people often feel happier if you smile at them?

3 **What about you? In pairs, ask and answer.**

   1 In what situations do people in your country smile at people they don't know?

   2 How do you feel if someone gives you a fake smile?

   3 How do you cheer yourself up when you're in a bad mood?

   4 Think about something sad. Then think about the same thing and smile. Are your feelings the same or different?

What's in a Smile?

You can't hope to learn all the world's languages, but there's one language that you can communicate with everywhere: your smile.

Smiling can show people that you're friendly and cheerful. According to scientists, however, we have more than fifty different types of smile for different situations. When something is funny, we usually smile with an open mouth. If we are proud of something, we keep our lips together. If our eyes become smaller when we smile, we are genuinely happy, but if the skin around our eyes doesn't move, our smile is fake. That's bad news in countries where people dislike a fake smile as much as a frown, like France and Russia.

But what if you are in a bad mood? It's hard to be cheerful all the time. Some people try to cheer themselves up by watching funny movies. Others prefer dancing to their favorite songs or eating chocolate. Others do sports every day to put themselves in a good mood. But there's another, very easy way to feel happier: smile. When you smile (even if it's a fake smile), your body starts producing chemicals called endorphins. Endorphins send a message to your brain that you are happy. And there's more. When you smile at people, they often smile back at you. This reaction produces endorphins in their body, and they feel happier, too. A part of their brain remembers you as a person who makes them happy. You're halfway to having a new friend. And that's definitely something you can smile about.

Grammar • Gerunds and infinitives

Gerunds
1 They cheer themselves up by watching funny movies.
2 Smiling can show people that you're friendly.
3 They prefer dancing to their favorite songs.

Infinitives
4 You can't hope to learn all the world's languages.
5 They do sports every day to put themselves in a good mood.
6 It's hard to be cheerful all the time.

Grammar reference page 114

1 Study the grammar table. Match the examples (1–6) to the uses (a–f).

We use **gerunds**:
a after certain verbs, e.g., *like, love, enjoy, hate, prefer, stop.*
b after prepositions.
c as the subject or object of a sentence.

We use **infinitives**:
d after certain verbs, e.g., *want, decide, hope, try, pretend, learn, remember, plan.*
e after certain adjectives, e.g., *easy, difficult, important, happy, sad, lucky.*
f when we are explaining the purpose of an action.

2 Choose the correct options.

Here are some of your ideas for [1] *being* / *to be* happy:

☺ [2] *Spending* / *To spend* time with my friends always makes me happy.

☺ Try [3] *not wanting* / *not to want* expensive gadgets. They can't bring you real happiness.

☺ I often go running [4] *escaping* / *to escape* my problems. I always feel better after a run.

☺ Remember [5] *not being* / *not to be* selfish. It's easier [6] *becoming* / *to become* happy by [7] *helping* / *to help* other people.

☺ I enjoy [8] *watching* / *to watch* comedies on TV. It's impossible [9] *frowning* / *to frown* when you're laughing!

3 Complete the sentences with the correct form of the verbs.

1 It's important *to have* (have) good friends.
2 Are you hoping .... (go) on vacation soon?
3 I hate .... (not be) at the same school as my sister.
4 Please stop .... (shout). You're giving me a headache!
5 It's hard .... (not feel) a little jealous of Lucy. She's so popular!
6 They want .... (relax) this weekend.
7 She's going to London .... (visit) her grandparents.
8 .... (play) table tennis is a lot of fun.

4 Complete the text with the correct form of these verbs.

do	feel	go	leave
meet	start	talk	~~work~~

Two years ago, my parents were tired of [1] *working* for big companies in New York. They decided [2] .... their jobs. We moved to a new home in the mountains [3] .... a new life. At first I didn't enjoy [4] .... to my new school. No one in my class wanted [5] .... to me. Then I joined the school's mountain sports club. I learned [6] .... sports like rock climbing and skiing, and it was easier [7] .... friendly people in the club. Soon I stopped [8] .... unhappy, and now I love my new home.

5 What about you? In pairs, ask and answer.

1 Which activities do you enjoy/not like doing?
2 What things are easy/difficult to do?
3 What are your plans and hopes for next year?

Bhutan

Bhutan is a small but beautiful country in the Himalayas. Its people are not wealthy—they live on less than five dollars a day. But they feel lucky. They have a king who tries to make them happy, not rich, and he is very successful. The Bhutanese are famous for being the happiest people in all of Asia.

They believe that people can't be happy if they aren't healthy, so Bhutan has good hospitals. It doesn't want factories that pollute the environment with poisonous chemicals. Before 1999, the king thought that TV was a dangerous influence and didn't allow it. Today people can watch TV, but there is more crime now in this peaceful country.

Vocabulary • Adjective suffixes

1 Read the article and find the adjective forms of these nouns. Copy and complete the table. Then listen, check and repeat.

1.31

| ~~beauty~~ | danger | fame | health | luck |
| peace | poison | success | wealth | |

	Noun	Adjective
-ful	beauty	beautiful
-y	....	....
-ous	....	....

Word list page 43
Workbook page 120

2 Complete the sentences with words from Exercise 1.

1 There is no crime in this town. It's a very *peaceful* place.
2 Mom wished me good .... before the exam.
3 There are a lot of road accidents. Driving a car can be really .... .
4 He is so .... that he has a yacht!
5 She has a .... face, but she isn't tall enough to be a model.
6 Everyone knows Tom Cruise. He's a .... actor.
7 Don't eat those mushrooms. They're .... !
8 He has won a lot of races, but his .... in sports hasn't made him rich or famous.
9 She's very ....—she plays tennis every day and eats a lot of fruit.

3 In pairs, take turns saying a noun from Exercise 1. Your partner makes a sentence with the adjective form of the noun.

luck

My uncle is very lucky. He always wins money in the lottery.

Brain Trainer Unit 3
Activity 3
Go to page 60

Chatroom Invitations

Speaking and Listening

1 Look at the photo. How is Fraser feeling? Why?

2 Listen and read the conversation.
1.32 Check your answer.

3 Listen and read again. Answer the questions.
1.32
1 Why can't Archie and Holly go to the youth club?
Because they're going to Yasmin's party.
2 Why isn't Fraser going to the party?
3 Why does Yasmin call Fraser?
4 Why did Yasmin think she had invited Fraser to her party?
5 What does Fraser decide to do tonight?

4 Act out the conversation in groups of four.

Fraser	Do you want to go to the youth club tonight?
Archie	That sounds like fun, but I'm sorry, I can't. I'm going to Yasmin's party.
Fraser	What about you, Holly? Do you feel like going?
Holly	Sorry. I have to say no, too. Yasmin's been planning her party for months. It's going to be a great night.
Fraser	It's not fair! I didn't even get an invitation … Oh, that's my phone. Hello?
Yasmin	Fraser, hi, it's Yasmin. I've been calling you all day, but you never answer. Are you coming to my party? You haven't replied yet.
Fraser	Well, you haven't invited me yet.
Yasmin	Really? I thought I sent you a text last week.
Fraser	I didn't get one.
Yasmin	Oh, I'm such a lost cause! Sorry. Well, would you like to come? It's tonight at 7:30.
Fraser	Sure! Thanks. I'll see you there.

Say it in your language …
It's not fair!
I'm such a lost cause!

5 Look back at the conversation. Who says what?

1 Do you want to go to the youth club? *Fraser*
2 Do you feel like going?
3 Sure! Thanks. I'll see you there.
4 Sorry. I have to say no.
5 Would you like to come?
6 That sounds like fun, but I'm sorry, I can't.

6 Read the phrases for inviting, and accepting and declining invitations.

Inviting
Do you want to …?
Would you like to …?
Do you feel like … *-ing*?

Accepting
That's a great idea. I'd love to!
Sure! Thanks. I'll see you there.

Declining
That sounds like fun, but I'm sorry, I can't.
Sorry. I have to say no.

7 Listen to the conversations. Who accepts
1.33 the invitation? Who declines it? Act out the conversations.

Archie Do you feel like [1] going to the movies later?
Fraser That sounds like fun, but I'm sorry, I can't. I have [2] too much homework.

Holly Hello. Would you like to [1] play computer games at my house on Friday night?
Fraser Sorry. I have to say no. [2] My mom's birthday dinner is on Friday.

Yasmin Hi! Do you want to [1] go to a rock concert with me tonight?
Holly That's a great idea. I'd love to!

Archie Do you feel like [1] having lunch at my house on Saturday?
Yasmin Sure! Thanks. I'll see you there.

8 Work in pairs. Replace the words in purple in Exercise 7. Use these words and/or your own ideas. Act out the conversations.

1 meet(ing) in the park / go(ing) out for a pizza / see(ing) a horror movie

2 my guitar lesson / my cousin's party

Grammar • Present perfect continuous

How long **has** she **been planning** her party?

She **has been planning** her party for months.

She **hasn't been planning** her party for very long.

Grammar reference page 114

1 Study the grammar table. Choose the correct options to complete the rules.

1 We form the Present perfect continuous with *have* (or *has*) + *been* + verb + *-ing* / *-ed*.
2 We use this tense for a *short and sudden* / *longer* action that started in the past and *continues* / *doesn't continue* until the present.
3 The action *might* / *won't* continue in the future.

2 Complete the sentences with the Present perfect continuous form of the verbs in parentheses.

1 How long *has she been standing* (she/stand) there?
2 I …. (not have) a good time at my new school.
3 He's sweating because he …. (run) for two hours.
4 …. (he/do) homework this morning?
5 They …. (not learn) French for very long.
6 She's very upset. She …. (cry) for 20 minutes.
7 There's a horrible smell in the kitchen! What …. (you/cook)?
8 He's shivering because he …. (swim), and the water's very cold.

3 Complete the sentences. Use the Present perfect continuous.

1 I'm really good at English now. I …. .
2 There's green paint in your hair. What …. ?
3 They're very tired. They …. .
4 Your sister's awesome at soccer. How long …. ?
5 This is such a long car trip! We …. .
6 He doesn't know many people in this town because he …. .
7 She's talking to Max on the phone. They …. .
8 We've been in the library. We …. .

Reading

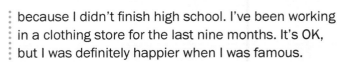

1 Read the article quickly. Which person:

1 was a famous singer? *James*
2 had a celebrity boyfriend?
3 is happy to stay in the background?
4 misses his/her fame?

Most young people dream of being famous, and with all the reality shows and talent contests on TV, it has never been easier to achieve that dream. But does fame bring happiness?

Melanie Greening

I was in a successful reality show when I was eighteen, and I got a job as a TV host after that. My boyfriend was a famous soccer player, and we were in the newspapers all the time. We went to the coolest parties. Life was fantastic! But I wasn't very good at hosting TV shows. I lost my job, and then my boyfriend left me. One month I was a star, and the next I was a nobody. No one recognized me in the street anymore. People have such short memories! It wasn't easy to find another job

because I didn't finish high school. I've been working in a clothing store for the last nine months. It's OK, but I was definitely happier when I was famous.

James Levy

I won a TV singing contest when I was sixteen. I was thrilled, but that didn't last long. I was so busy with recording sessions, TV appearances, concerts and photo shoots that I never had time to relax. I really missed my family. They lived far away, so I couldn't see them very often. And the fans were a problem, too. Every time I went out, people used to scream because they were excited to see me. They put their arms around me for a photo, or pushed a pen into my hand so I could sign something for them. One sent me a poisonous spider as a birthday present! Now I write songs, and other people sing them. I still love the music industry. But fame? No, thanks. I prefer a more peaceful life.

Key Words	
talent contest	TV host
recognize	recording session
TV appearance	photo shoot

2 Read the article again. Are the statements true (T), false (F) or don't know (DK)?

1.34

1 Melanie worked for a newspaper. *F*
2 She earned a lot of money when she was famous.
3 People forgot Melanie very quickly after she lost her job.
4 She didn't do well at school.
5 After James won the contest, he had too much free time.
6 He wanted to see his family more often.
7 It was hard to make new friends when he was famous.
8 He enjoyed all the attention from his fans.

Listening

1 Listen to the interview with Luke Evans. Are the

1.35 statements true (T) or false (F)?

1 Luke is an actor.
2 He has been famous since he was five.
3 He's had a crazy life.

 Listening Bank Unit 3 page 61

2 In pairs, ask and answer.

1 Do you know about the lives of any child stars?
2 Do you think child stars are lucky? Why?/Why not?
3 Would you like to be famous? Why?/Why not?

Writing • A "for and against" essay

1 Read the Writing File.

> **Writing File** Linking words: addition and contrast
>
> **You can introduce additional ideas with *and*, *also*, *too* and *additionally*.**
>
> I was in a talent contest and I won.
> He's an actor. He's also a TV host.
> They can sing. They can dance, too.
> She's very beautiful. Additionally, she's a very good actor.
>
> **You can introduce contrasting ideas with *but*, *however* and *on the other hand*.**
>
> She's a nurse, but she wants to be a singer.
> He's learning to dance. However, he's not good at it.
> Famous singers often come from poor families. On the other hand, a number of singers have wealthy parents.

2 Answer the questions.

1 Which words go at the beginning of a sentence?
2 Which word goes after the first or second word in a sentence?
3 Which words go in the middle of a sentence?
4 Which word goes at the end of a sentence?

3 Complete the sentences with a word or phrase from the Writing File.

1 My brother's a baseball player. My boyfriend's *also* a baseball player.
2 I like rap music. .... , I don't like jazz.
3 He's been practicing all day, and he's going to practice this evening, ...
4 Living in a city has some advantages. .... , there are some disadvantages.
5 I'm happy to help, ... I don't have much time.
6 Child stars have an exciting life. .... , they earn a lot of money.
7 Robert Pattinson was in one of the Harry Potter movies, ... then he was in the *Twilight* movies.

4 Read the essay. Find the linking words.

Wealth Makes People Happy

Many people dream of being rich, <u>but</u> does wealth make people happy?

Rich people certainly don't have the same worries as poor people. They can easily pay for a comfortable home and enough food. They have more choices than ordinary people, too. For example, they don't have to have a job. They can also afford designer clothes and exciting vacations.

On the other hand, good relationships with friends and family are more important than clothes and vacations. It's difficult to know if your friends are genuine if you are rich. Perhaps they are pretending to like you to get some of your money. Additionally, expensive things soon seem ordinary if you can buy them all the time.

In conclusion, rich people definitely have a happier life than very poor people. However, I don't think rich people are always truly happy. The happiest people are in the middle—neither rich nor poor.

5 Read the essay again and complete the notes.

> Advantages of being rich
> They can pay for [1]a comfortable home and [2] .... .
> They don't have to have [3] .... .
> They can afford [4] .... and [5] .... .
> Disadvantages of being rich
> They don't know if their friends are [6] .... .
> Expensive things seem [7] .... to them.
> Conclusion
> The [8] .... people are not rich and not poor.

6 You are going to write an essay with the title *Fame Makes People Happy*. Take notes on the advantages and disadvantages of being famous.

7 Write your essay. Use the notes in Exercise 5 and the structure of the essay in Exercise 4 to help you.

> **Remember!**
> • Use linking words.
> • Use the vocabulary in this unit.
> • Check your grammar, spelling and punctuation.

Refresh Your Memory!

Grammar • Review

1 **Choose the correct options.**

1 I'm lucky *having* / *to have* friends who live near my house.
2 I want *watching* / *to watch* a horror movie at home tonight.
3 Stop *being* / *to be* so rude.
4 She went there *helping* / *to help* her cousin.
5 They were pretending *not recognizing* / *not to recognize* me.
6 *Living* / *To live* at the beach is a lot of fun.
7 We're talking about *going* / *to go* on summer vacation together.

2 **Complete the sentences with the correct form of the verbs.**

1 It's impossible *to surf* (surf) when there aren't any waves.
2 I'm going to Miami …. (learn) English.
3 He apologized for …. (forget) my birthday.
4 I hate …. (not have) a cell phone.
5 Remember …. (not get) home late tonight.
6 She insisted on …. (pay) for everyone's tickets.
7 He isn't planning …. (finish) school next year.
8 …. (laugh) is the quickest way to feel happier.

3 **Complete the conversation with the Present perfect continuous form of the verbs.**

A Oh, Jack, there you are! Mom ¹ *has been looking* (look) for you. She ² …. (shout) your name for about ten minutes.
B Oh, sorry. I didn't hear. I ³ …. (listen) to music in the backyard.
A What else ⁴ …. (you/do) out there? Your hands are red. ⁵ …. (you/use) red paint?
B No. I ⁶ …. (not paint). I ⁷ …. (talk) to Carrie, and we ⁸ …. (eat) strawberries.
A Well, wash your hands and find Mom. She ⁹ …. (work) all day, and she's tired. She needs your help.

Vocabulary • Review

4 **Complete the sentences with these words.**

blushed	cried	gasped
~~laughed~~	shivered	yawned

1 Everyone *laughed* at his joke.
2 She …. in amazement when she heard the news.
3 I …. when I walked out into the snow.
4 She …. for days when her boyfriend left her.
5 I …. when I saw the embarrassing photo.
6 He …. . It was late, and he was tired.

5 **Complete the text with the adjective form of the words.**

Most of us want to become ¹ *wealthy* and live in a big, ² …. house, but it isn't easy to get rich. ³ …. actors are rich, but most actors are never ⁴ …. . You could start a business, but it isn't a ⁵ …. life. It's better not to want a lot of money. If you are ⁶ …. , live in a place that isn't ⁷ …. and have good friends and enough food, you are a ⁸ …. person.

WEALTH
BEAUTY
FAME
SUCCESS
PEACE

HEALTH
DANGER
LUCK

Speaking • Review

6 **Make questions and answers.**
1.36 **Then listen and check.**

1 **A** you / feel like / go / to the park / ?
   Do you feel like going to the park?
   B I / be / sorry / I / can't
2 **A** you / like / come / to my house / ?
   B great idea / love to / !
3 **A** you / want / meet / downtown / later / ?
   B Sorry / have / say no

Dictation

7 **Listen and write in your notebook.**
1.37

✓ My assessment profile: page 132

Operation Smile

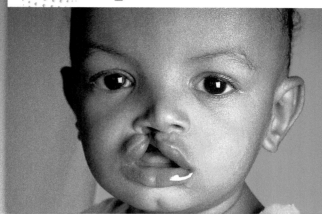

Every three minutes, a child is born with a cleft lip or cleft palate. Children with these conditions have terrible problems with eating, drinking and speaking, and one in ten of them dies before the age of one. The luckier ones live, but they are often rejected by friends and sometimes even by their own families.

In rich countries, simple surgical operations can correct most of these mouth problems and allow children to live normal lives. But in poorer countries, the operations are too expensive for most people, and not enough surgeons are available to do them.

Reading

1 **Read the article quickly. Are the statements true (T) or false (F)?**

1 Operation Smile is a charity. *T*
2 It helps children with medical problems.
3 Most of its work is in the US.
4 All its volunteers are doctors and nurses.

2 **Read the article again and answer the questions.**

1.38 1 Why are cleft lips and cleft palates dangerous?
Because children can have terrible problems with eating, drinking and speaking.
2 Why is it difficult to have these operations in some countries?
3 Why did the Magees start Operation Smile?
4 What three things does Operation Smile do?
5 How can students go on an Operation Smile trip?

In 1982 Bill Magee, an American doctor, and his wife Kathy, a nurse, went to the Philippines to do some cleft palate surgeries. But it was a short trip, and there wasn't time to help all the children who needed surgery. They felt terribly guilty. When they got home, they started a new charity. They called it Operation Smile.

Operation Smile now works in more than sixty countries. Five thousand volunteers give their time and skills to provide free mouth surgery to the children who need it most. The charity also provides medical equipment and trains local doctors to do the surgery themselves. In this way, the results of an Operation Smile visit continue long into the future.

When an international group of doctors and nurses travels to a country, two high school students go, too. The students usually have done a lot of fundraising in their local area and told a lot of people about the work of Operation Smile. Their trip is a fantastic way to experience a completely different culture and help to change lives forever.

3 **Listen to the interview. Copy and complete**
1.39 **the report.**

Name	Marisa Correa
Country visited	....
Length of trip	.... days
Work	Taught children and parents about staying .... and taking care of .... .
Enjoyed trip?	Yes / No
Number of operations	....

My Global Citizenship File

4 **Find out about another important charity that teenagers can help. Answer these questions.**

- What work does it do?
- Why is its work important?
- What can teenagers do to help?
- What do teenagers say about their experiences with the charity?

5 **Make a poster for the charity, advertising for teenage volunteers.**

Grammar • Past simple/Past continuous

1 Choose the correct options.

Yesterday I [1] *visited / was visiting* my cousins in New Haven. When I [2] *arrived / was arriving* at their house, they [3] *listened / were listening* to music in their room. We [4] *didn't have / weren't having* lunch at their house. We [5] *took / were taking* the bus to Church Street. While we [6] *ate / were eating* lunch at the diner, we [7] *saw / were seeing* the actor Claire Danes.

2 Make sentences.

1 We / walk to school / when / my sister / drop / her camera on the ground
We were walking to school when my sister dropped her camera on the ground.

2 While / Bob / talk on the phone / he / hear / a loud noise outside

3 My friends / play Frisbee / in the park / when / it / start / to rain

4 Nina / sprain / her ankle / while / she / run / in the backyard

5 My brother / see / a robbery / while / he / work / in the supermarket

• Used to

3 Look at the notes. Make sentences about what people used to do and didn't use to do in the 1980s.

In the 1980s	
✗	**✓**
send emails	send faxes
watch DVDs	watch videos
have cell phones	use public pay phones
use computers at home	use typewriters

In the 1980s, people didn't use to send emails; they used to send faxes.

• Present perfect + *ever, never, already, yet*

4 Choose the correct options.

1 I've *never / ever* eaten Japanese food.
2 Have you eaten your lunch *yet / ever*?
3 I've *already / never* cleaned up my room, but I haven't walked the dog *yet / already*.
4 This is the funniest joke I've *ever / already* heard!

5 Complete the sentences with *for* or *since*.

1 We've lived in this house *for* six years.
2 Greg's had the same bike .... 2012.
3 .... she was a child, Nora's been a fan of basketball.
4 I haven't seen Adam .... a while! Is he OK?

6 Complete the sentences. Use the Present perfect.

1 *Have* you *ever met* (ever/meet) a famous person?
2 My mother .... (never fly) in a plane.
3 **A** Do you want a sandwich?
    B No, thanks. I .... (already/eat) lunch.
4 .... you .... this book .... ? (read/yet)

• Present perfect/Past simple

7 Make questions in the Present perfect and answers in the Past simple.

1 you / ever / win a prize?
yes / win / singing contest / two years ago
Have you ever won a prize?
Yes. I won a singing contest two years ago.

2 you / see / the new James Bond movie?
yes / see / it / last weekend

3 your parents / buy / a new car?
yes / buy / a Volkswagen / on Saturday

4 Peter / lose / his new phone?
yes / lose / it / at the party last night

8 Complete the text with the Present perfect or Past simple form of the verbs.

My sister [1] *'s already come* (already/come) back from France. She [2] .... (go) there on vacation with her friends, Jenny and Sarah. They [3] .... (stay) in a hotel in Paris. I [4] .... (never/visit) France, but I [5] .... (just/read) a really interesting book about the Eiffel Tower.

Gerunds and infinitives

9 **Choose the correct options.**

1 It's difficult *to review / reviewing* for exams in the summer because I like *to be / being* outside with my friends, and I don't want *to read / reading* books in my room.

2 I used my new camera *to take / taking* this photo of my dog. He was trying *to catch / catching* a rabbit.

3 It's important not *to get / getting* angry when you can't do something. Remember *to try / trying* hard, and don't be afraid of *to fail / failing*.

10 **Complete the text with the infinitive or gerund form of the verbs.**

I hope ¹ *to spend* (spend) the summer at the beach. I love ² .... (swim), and I also enjoy ³ .... (play) beach volleyball. My brother, however, prefers ⁴ .... (go) on activity vacations. He's decided ⁵ .... (travel) with our cousin this summer. They're planning ⁶ .... (take) the train to Scotland and then go mountain climbing.

Present perfect continuous

11 **Make questions and answers in the Present perfect continuous.**

1 How long / you / wait / here
I / wait / here / for half an hour
How long have you been waiting here?
I've been waiting here for half an hour.

2 How long / your sister / learn / Chinese
She / learn / Chinese / since 2011

3 How long / Jess and Emma / work / at this café
They / work / at this café / for three months

4 How long / we / stand / on this platform
We / stand / on this platform / for 40 minutes

12 **Complete the text with the Present perfect continuous form of the verbs.**

I just got my black belt in judo! I ¹ *'ve been practicing* (practice) martial arts for ten years, but I ² .... (not/study) judo for very long. My dad ³ .... (teach) judo since 2007. My friends ⁴ .... (come) to his classes with me recently, and we ⁵ .... (watch) martial arts movies together afterward.

Speaking • Expressing extremes

1 **Complete the conversation with these words.**

| really amazing | really awful | ~~so good~~ |
| such a great | such a terrible | |

A Your brother's very talented. He's ¹ *so good* at music.
B Yes, he's written some ² .... songs.
A And he's ³ .... pianist as well.
B That's true. But he's a ⁴ .... singer.
A I didn't know that!
B Yes, he has ⁵ .... voice!
A Oh no!

Giving/Responding to news

2 **Complete the conversation.**

A ¹ *What's up,* Dan?
B I ² j .... h .... the most incredible news.
A What ³ h .... ?
B You won't ⁴ b .... it, but my brother has won the regional under-16 diving competition.
A You're ⁵ k .... m .... !
B ⁶ S ..... . My mom just called me. He's made it to the national finals!

Invitations

3 **Put the conversation in the correct order.**

☐ a That sounds like fun, but I'm sorry, I can't. I have a tennis lesson this afternoon.

☐ b Do you want to meet me at the corner store on Hill Street at 6 o'clock? Then we can buy some popcorn and eat it at home while we're watching the movie.

☐ c That's a great idea. I'd love to!

☐ d Sure. Thanks. I'll see you there.

☐1☐ e Hi, Katie. Do you feel like going to the park this afternoon?

☐ f Oh well, would you like to come to my house later this evening? We can watch a DVD.

Vocabulary • Compound nouns

1 **Complete the compound nouns in the sentences.**

1 My father used to be a *business* person in the city, but now he works as a ....fighter in a small town.
2 When we went to New York, we saw a lot of sky.... .
3 The speed.... was racing through the water when the pilot saw the light.... .
4 We traveled fast through the snow on our snow.... .
5 My ....mates and I copied the information about our ....work from the white.... .
6 My little sister goes to a baby.... after school because my parents work until 6 p.m.
7 That isn't a space.... in the sky—it's a balloon!
8 The old wind.... just outside our town still makes flour for the local baker.

• Phrasal verbs 1

2 **Choose the correct options.**

1 My friends often hang *out / off* at the mall on the weekend, but I can't—my mom counts *on / of* me to watch my little brother.
2 You have to fill *up / out* this form before you set *out / up* your own business.
3 I'm looking *for / about* my cat. He ran *away / out* yesterday.
4 I give *away / up*! I want to find *up / out* some information for my geography project, but my computer isn't working.
5 When we get *before / back* from vacation, I will go *out / up* with my friends.

• Collocations with *make*, *go* and *keep*

3 **Find the word or phrase that doesn't fit.**

1 keep *a secret / together / control*
2 make *crazy / a difference / it to the finals*
3 keep *calm / a difference / in touch*
4 go *for a walk / a dream come true / out*
5 make *in touch / someone's dream come true / a decision*
6 go *crazy / together / control*

• Jobs and suffixes *-or, -er, -ist*

4 **Copy the table and complete the list.**

things	jobs
art	*artist*
....	novelist
....	photographer
play	....
poem	....
....	sculptor

• Showing feelings

5 **Complete the sentences with the correct form of these verbs.**

~~blush~~	frown	gasp	laugh	scream
shiver	smile	sweat	yawn	

1 She was embarrassed, so she *blushed*.
2 The girl .... loudly at my joke.
3 He's very tired. He's ..... .
4 When it's hot, we .... , and when it's cold, we .... .
5 She .... with surprise when the door opened and then .... in terror when she saw the ghost.
6 He is .... because he's in a bad mood at the moment, but when he's happy, he always .... .

• Adjective suffixes

6 **Put the letters in the correct order to complete the adjectives.**

1 u b i a e t   *beauti*ful
2 e l h h a t   _ _ _ _ _ _ y
3 a m f   _ _ _ ous
4 e a w h l t   _ _ _ _ _ _ y
5 s n o i p o   _ _ _ _ _ _ ous
6 k l u c   _ _ _ _ y
7 c s c s e s u   _ _ _ _ _ _ ful
8 c p a e e   _ _ _ _ _ ful
9 g d a n e r   _ _ _ _ _ _ ous

Word list 🔊

Unit 1 • Different Lives

Compound nouns

babysitter	/ˈbeɪbiˌsɪtɚ/
business person	/ˈbɪznɪsˈˌpɚsən/
classmate	/ˈklæsmeɪt/
firefighter	/ˈfaɪɚˌfaɪt̬ɚ/
homework	/ˈhoʊmwɚk/
lighthouse	/ˈlaɪthaʊs/
skyscraper	/ˈskaɪˌskreɪpɚ/
snowmobile	/ˈsnoʊmoʊˌbil/
spaceship	/ˈspeɪsˌʃɪp/
speedboat	/ˈspidboʊt/
whiteboard	/ˈwaɪtbɔrd/
windmill	/ˈwɪndˌmɪl/

Phrasal verbs

count on	/ˈkaʊnt ɔn/
fill out	/ˌfɪl ˈaʊt/
find out	/ˌfaɪnd ˈaʊt/
get back	/ˌgɛt ˈbæk/
give up	/ˌgɪv ˈʌp/
go out	/ˌgo ˈaʊt/
hang out	/ˌhæŋ ˈaʊt/
look for	/ˌlʊk ˈfɔr/
run away	/ˌrʌn əˈweɪ/
set up	/ˌsɛt ˈʌp/

Unit 2 • Aiming High

Collocations with *make, go* and *keep*

go crazy	/ˌgoʊ ˈkreɪzi/
go for a walk	/ˌgoʊ fɚ ə ˈwɔk/
go together	/ˌgoʊ təˈgɛðɚ/
go well	/ˌgoʊ ˈwɛl/
keep a secret	/ˌkip ə ˈsikrɪt/
keep calm	/ˌkip ˈkɑm/
keep control	/ˌkip kənˈtroʊl/
keep in touch	/ˌkip ɪn ˈtʌtʃ/
make a decision	/ˌmeɪk ə dɪˈsɪʒən/
make a difference	/ˌmeɪk ə ˈdɪfrəns/
make it to the finals	/ˌmeɪk ɪt tə ðə ˈfaɪnəlz/
make someone's dream come true	/ˌmeɪk ˈsʌmwʌnz ˌdrim ˈkʌm ˈtru/

Jobs and suffixes *-or, -er, -ist*

Common stative verbs (see page 12)				
be	believe	belong	cost	feel
get	hate	have	hear	know
like	love	need	own	see
smell	taste	think	understand	want

art	/ɑrt/
artist	/ˈɑrt̬ɪst/
novel	/ˈnɑvəl/
novelist	/ˈnɑvəlɪst/
photograph	/ˈfoʊt̬əˌgræf/
photographer	/fəˈtɑgrəfɚ/
play	/pleɪ/
playwright	/ˈpleɪraɪt/
poem	/ˈpoʊəm/
poet	/ˈpoʊɪt/
sculptor	/ˈskʌlptɚ/
sculpture	/ˈskʌlptʃɚ/

Unit 3 • Be Happy!

Showing feelings

blush	/blʌʃ/
cry	/kraɪ/
frown	/fraʊn/
gasp	/gæsp/
laugh	/læf/
scream	/skrim/
shiver	/ˈʃɪvɚ/
shout	/ʃaʊt/
sigh	/saɪ/
smile	/smaɪl/
sweat	/swɛt/
yawn	/yɔn/

Adjective suffixes

beautiful	/ˈbyut̬əfəl/
dangerous	/ˈdeɪndʒərəs/
famous	/ˈfeɪməs/
healthy	/ˈhɛlθi/
lucky	/ˈlʌki/
peaceful	/ˈpisfəl/
poisonous	/ˈpɔɪzənəs/
successful	/səkˈsɛsfəl/
wealthy	/ˈwɛlθi/

4 Survive!

Vocabulary • Natural disasters

1 **Match sentences (1–9) to photos (a–i). Then listen, check and repeat.**

2.1

1 When **volcanoes erupt**, they are dangerous. *i*
2 **Earthquakes** can **destroy** buildings.
3 People sometimes **drown** in **floods**.
4 A **disease** can **spread** very quickly.
5 In a **famine**, people sometimes **starve**.
6 An **avalanche** can **bury** you under snow.
7 Most plants can't **survive** in a **drought**.
8 A **hurricane** is a storm with very strong winds.
9 A **tsunami** is a huge, dangerous wave.

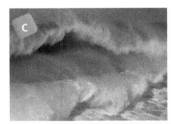

2 **Complete the sentences with the correct form of the**
2.2 **words in bold in Exercise 1. Then listen and check.**

1 In the story of Noah's Ark, there was a great *flood*.
2 Mount Vesuvius is a .... that .... in AD 79 and .... the Roman city of Pompeii under five meters of ash.
3 A lot of people .... on the *Titanic* in 1912. Wealthy passengers were more likely to .... .
4 60,000 men died in an .... in the Alps in World War I.
5 6,000,000 people .... in a .... in Ukraine in the 1930s.
6 The world's longest .... was in the Atacama Desert in Chile. It didn't rain there for 400 years.
7 An .... near the coast of Japan in 2011 caused a terrible .... . The disaster killed more than 15,000 people and .... more than 300,000 buildings.
8 .... Katrina devastated New Orleans in 2005.
9 Malaria is a .... that mosquitoes .... .

3 **In pairs, ask and answer.**

1 Have there been any natural disasters in your country? What happened?
2 What natural disasters have happened in other countries? What can you remember about them?

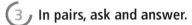
2.3, 2.4 **Pronunciation Unit 4** page 63

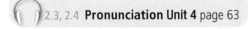
**Brain Trainer Unit 4
Activities 1 and 2**
Go to page 60

Reading

1 **Look at the photos. Answer the questions.**

1 What part of the world do you think this is?
2 What bad news does the article give?
3 What good news does it give?

2 **Read the article quickly and check your answers.**

3 **Match sentences (1–4) to blanks (A–D) in the article.**

1 It came in 2007.
2 Not everyone in Bangladesh was so lucky.
3 It was one of the worst natural disasters of the twentieth century.
4 "You must come to the school now," they shouted.

4 **Read the article again. Are the statements true (T) or false (F)?**

2.5

1 Because of global warming, there are more natural disasters now than there were in the past. *T*
2 The cyclone in 1991 was stronger than the cyclone in 1970.
3 The cyclone in 1991 killed more people than the cyclone in 1970.
4 In 1991 there was nowhere safe for women and children to go.
5 A scientist in the US helped to save lives in Cyclone Sidr.
6 The buildings in Rupa's village survived because of the cyclone warning.

5 **What about you? In pairs, ask and answer.**

1 Are there ever floods in your country? What problems do they cause?
2 What do people do to prepare for natural disasters in your country? Do you think they do enough?
3 Many charities say "There are more floods and droughts now because of global warming. Rich countries should pay the poor countries affected by these problems." Why do they say this? Do you agree? Why?/Why not?

Fighting Disasters

Every year, natural disasters affect about 250 million people. Global warming is making droughts, floods and avalanches more common. We can't stop the disasters, but we can reduce the number of people who die in them.

In Bangladesh, a lot of people have to live on flat land near the ocean, but strong winds, called cyclones in this part of the world, bring terrible floods. In 1970 Cyclone Bhola killed about 500,000 people. **A** .... In 1991 the even stronger Cyclone Gorky hit the country. This time, people could use special school buildings as emergency shelters. Unfortunately, many women and children didn't go to them, and around 140,000 people drowned.

After this, villages set up groups of emergency volunteers, and teachers had to talk to children every week about the things they should do if there was a cyclone warning.

They didn't have to wait many years for the next big cyclone. **B** *1* Twelve hours before Cyclone Sidr reached land, a Bangladeshi scientist in the US used a computer to calculate the exact areas of danger. The emergency volunteers in the villages spread the warning fast.

Ten-year-old Rupa Begum and her friends ran to all their neighbors' homes. **C** .... "You won't be safe if you stay here." All the buildings in the village were destroyed in the disaster, except for the school shelter. Thanks to the children's warnings, everyone in the village survived.

D .... Four thousand people died in Cyclone Sidr. But this was a much smaller number than in the big cyclones of the twentieth century. With modern technology, planning and education, we don't have to lose huge numbers of lives in natural disasters.

Grammar • Modals: ability, obligation, prohibition, advice

Ability
We can reduce the number of people who die.
We can't stop natural disasters.

Obligation
You must come to the school now.
They have to live on flat land near the ocean.
We don't have to lose huge numbers of lives.

Prohibition
You mustn't leave the shelter.

Advice
You should listen to the warnings.
You shouldn't go near the ocean.

Grammar reference page 116

1 Study the grammar table. Choose the correct options to complete the rules.

1 We use *must* or *have to* when an action is *necessary / against the rules.*
2 We use *don't have to* when an action is *impossible for someone / not necessary.*
3 We use *should* when an action is *a good idea / impossible for someone.*
4 We use *can* when an action is *not necessary / possible* for someone.
5 We use *mustn't* when an action is *a good idea / against the rules.*

2 Choose the correct options.

1 The mountains are popular because people *can / must* ski and climb there.
2 You *have to / mustn't* do mountain sports alone.
3 You *should / can't* check the weather before you go into the mountains.
4 People *must / shouldn't* go on the snow when there's a danger of avalanches.
5 If you are buried in an avalanche, you *don't have to / can't* get out. The snow is too heavy.
6 You *have to / don't have to* wait for help.

3 Choose the correct option, A, B, C or D, to complete the conversation.

Dad You look tired. You ¹ *D (should)* go to bed.
Bill I ² .... go to bed yet. I ³ .... to study French.
Dad Your French test isn't tomorrow; it's on Friday. You ⁴ .... study tonight. You ⁵ .... study another day.
Bill No, I ⁶ .... do it tonight, because I'm busy for the rest of the week. And I ⁷ .... get a bad grade on in the test.
Dad You ⁸ .... worry so much. Tonight sleep is more important than the test!

1 **A** shouldn't   **C** can't
   B mustn't   **D** should
2 **A** can   **C** can't
   B should   **D** must
3 **A** have   **C** shouldn't
   B must   **D** can
4 **A** don't have to   **C** can't
   B mustn't   **D** don't have
5 **A** mustn't   **C** doesn't have to
   B can   **D** can't
6 **A** must   **C** don't have
   B mustn't   **D** have
7 **A** should   **C** mustn't
   B must   **D** have to
8 **A** should   **C** shouldn't
   B must   **D** can

4 Make sentences. Change the underlined words. Use these words.

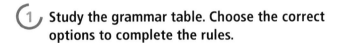

can	don't have to	has to	must
mustn't	~~should~~	shouldn't	

1 <u>It's a good idea to</u> get some exercise. (You)
   You should get some exercise.
2 I <u>have to</u> call Lucy. (I)
3 <u>It isn't necessary to</u> pay for the food. (You)
4 <u>It's against the rules to</u> use our cell phones in class. (We)
5 <u>It's a bad idea to</u> eat a lot of candy. (People)
6 <u>She's free to</u> go shopping on Saturday. (She)

5 What about you? **Discuss in pairs.**

1 rules at your school
2 rules at home
3 advice for someone who is new at your school

• Past modals

People could use schools as shelters.

I couldn't speak English when I was six.

They had to teach children about the dangers.

They didn't have to wait long for the next cyclone.

Grammar reference page 116

Watch Out!
We can't use *must* for obligation in the past.

6 **Study the grammar table. Complete the rules.**

> 1 For ability in the past, we use …. / …. .
> 2 For obligation in the past, we use …. / …. .

7 **Change these sentences to the past tense.**

1 She can't swim.
   She couldn't swim.
2 Can you see the avalanche?
3 They don't have to help us.
4 He must be careful.

Vocabulary • Phrasal verbs 2

1 **Read the text. Complete the phrasal verbs (1–10) and match them to their definitions (a–j). Then listen, check and repeat.**
2.6

1 break *down*	6 keep ….
2 calm ….	7 look ….
3 come ….	8 put ….
4 figure ….	9 run ….
5 get ….	10 take ….

a continue
b get dressed in something
c stop wearing something
d stop worrying
e stop working or functioning *1*
f come to the end of a difficult time
g be excited about something that's going to happen
h use all of something, so there isn't any more of it
i meet without planning to
j calculate or understand

Word list page 57   **Workbook** page 121

My Journal

I was looking forward to the sailing race, but after only three days of racing, the wind disappeared. Then my engine broke down, and the radio stopped working. I kept on trying to fix it, but I couldn't figure out what was wrong with it. The sun was very strong, so I took off my T-shirt and put it on my head. But then, while I was working on the engine, I fell and broke my leg. I was running out of drinking water, too. Could I get through this alive? Finally, I calmed down and waited quietly. After 24 hours, a boat came across mine and helped me to safety.

2 **Complete the sentences with the correct form of the words from Exercise 1.**

1 Stop screaming and *calm down*! We won't ….
   this if we don't think sensibly.
2 The car didn't …. . It …. gas.
3 …. looking at the map, and you'll ….
   our location soon.
4 I'm really …. the weekend. I'm going to Maine.
5 …. your dirty clothes, and …. some clean ones!
6 Today I …. an online ad for a volcano tour.

3 **Work in pairs. Choose six phrasal verbs from Exercise 1 and write a short conversation with them.**

Brain Trainer Unit 4
Activity 3
Go to page 60

Speaking and Listening

1 Look at the photo. Answer the questions.

1 Where are Archie, Holly and Yasmin?
2 What do you think just happened to Holly?
3 Who do you think Yasmin is talking to?

2 Listen and read the conversation.
2.7 Check your answers.

3 Listen and read again. Answer the questions.
2.7
1 What is wrong with Holly's foot?
  A snake bit it.
2 Does it hurt?
3 Is Archie worried about Holly? Why?/Why not?
4 Is an ambulance going to come?
5 Where does Holly have to go later?

4 Act out the conversation in groups of three.

Archie	Hurry up, guys!
Holly	We're coming … Ouch! What was that?
Yasmin	Oh no! A snake! Did it bite you?
Holly	Yes, on my foot.
Yasmin	Poor thing! That must really hurt!
Holly	Yes, and it could be really dangerous …
Archie	Calm down, Holly. It might be a poisonous snake, but it probably isn't deadly. There aren't that many deadly snakes in here.
Yasmin	I'll call the doctor. *(on phone)* Hello, my friend has a snake bite on her foot. What should we do? … Sorry, I don't understand. What do you mean? Are you saying that we should call for an ambulance, or keep on walking? … Oh, I see! Thanks.
Holly	What does the doctor think?
Yasmin	You have to go to the hospital. But we don't have to call an ambulance, so it can't be too serious.

Say it in your language …
Hurry up!
Ouch!

5 **Look back at the conversation. Complete these sentences.**

1 Sorry, I don't *understand*.
2 What do you .... ?
3 Are you .... that we should call for an ambulance, or keep on walking?
4 Oh, ... ! Thanks.

6 **Read the phrases for asking for clarification.**

Asking for clarification
What do you mean?
Sorry, I don't understand.
Are you saying that …?
Oh, I see! Thanks.

7 **Listen to the conversation. What is the problem and the solution? Act out the conversation in pairs.**
2.8

Archie You shouldn't ¹ swim in that river because of the ² water.
Yasmin Sorry, I don't understand. Are you saying that ³ the water is dangerous?
Archie Yes. So you shouldn't ⁴ swim in it.
Yasmin What do you mean?
Archie Well, ⁵ people have caught diseases here. You should ⁶ swim in a swimming pool.
Yasmin Oh, I see! Thanks.

8 **Work in pairs. Replace the words in purple in Exercise 7. Use these words and/or your own ideas. Act out the conversations.**

> You shouldn't ski there because of the snow.

> Sorry, I don't …

1 ski there / visit that volcano / keep food in your tent

2 snow / gas / bears

3 there's a problem with the snow / gas is coming from the volcano / there are bears around here

4 ski on it today / go there / keep food in your tent

5 there are often avalanches here / the gas is poisonous / bears steal food from tents

6 ski somewhere else / visit a different place / leave it in the campsite kitchen

Grammar • Modals: possibility

That bite must hurt.
It might be a poisonous snake.
The bite could be really dangerous.
The snake can't be deadly.
Grammar reference page 116

1 **Read the grammar table. Complete the rules.**

1 When something is possible, we use .... or .... .
2 When something is impossible, we use .... .
3 When something is certain, we use .... .

2 **Choose the correct options.**

A Where's Jackie?
B She isn't here. She ¹ *could* / *must* be in her tent, or she ² *might* / *can't* be down by the river.
A She ³ *must* / *can't* be in her tent. It's empty.
B Listen! Someone's yelling from the river. That ⁴ *must* / *can't* be her.
A She isn't yelling, she's screaming. She ⁵ *must* / *could* be scared!
B You're right. She ⁶ *might* / *can't* be in danger! Let's go and help her.

3 **Make two sentences for each picture. Use *must*, *might*, *could* or *can't*.**

1 Who is this? Jason and Luke both like surfing.
It might be Jason.
It could be Luke.

2 Where is this volcano? There aren't any volcanoes in Maryland, but there are some in Oregon.

3 What animal is that? Dolphins are gray, and sharks are gray, too.

Reading

1 Look at the photo and the title of the article. How do you think a television show saved this boy's life?

TV Saved My Life!

Teenager Jake Denham was skiing with his family in the US when he fell and lost one of his skis. His family didn't know that he had a problem. They kept on skiing. When they got to the bottom of the mountain, there was no sign of Jake.

Jake couldn't find his ski anywhere. In the end, he decided to take off his other ski and walk down the mountain. But he couldn't figure out the right way to go.

It was now getting dark, and he was a long way from any shelter. He knew that he might die that night in the cold temperatures. But Jake kept calm. At home, Jake watched a lot of TV shows about surviving in difficult situations. He remembered the advice from these shows and knew that he should build a cave in the snow. He made a hole and pointed it up the hill so the wind couldn't blow into it. Outside his cave, the temperature fell to a dangerous -15°C that night, but inside it Jake was safe from the cold.

But he had to get down the mountain. The TV shows always said, "If you are lost, you should find someone else's tracks through the snow and follow them." "I wanted to live my life," remembers Jake. "So I got up, and I found some ski tracks, and I followed those." He walked and walked, and finally he saw lights. Nine hours after he lost his ski, he came across a team of rescue workers. He was safe!

His mom was so relieved when she heard the news! Amazingly, Jake didn't even have to go to the hospital. He got through the ordeal without any injuries.

So, the next time someone says that watching TV is a waste of time, think of Jake. Sometimes TV can save your life!

Key Words

cave	hole	blow
track	rescue	ordeal

2 Read the article quickly and check your answer to Exercise 1.

3 2.9 Read the article again and put these events in the correct order. Which event didn't happen?

a He sheltered in a snow cave.
b He found rescuers.
c He fell. *1*
d He went to the hospital.
e He got lost.
f He followed ski tracks.

4 2.9 Read the article again. Answer the questions.

1 Why didn't Jake's family help him when he fell?
Because they didn't know he had a problem, and they kept on skiing.
2 At first, what did Jake plan to do?
3 Why was it dangerous for Jake when it got dark?
4 Why was his snow cave a good design?
5 How long was Jake lost on the mountain?
6 What injuries did Jake have?

Listening

1 2.10 Listen to a mountain rescue worker talk about survival shows on TV. Are the statements true (T) or false (F)?

1 They can help people.
2 They can give people dangerous ideas.
3 People should copy all the things that they see on survival shows.

 Listening Bank Unit 4 page 62

2 In pairs, discuss the questions. Give reasons.

1 Do you ever watch survival shows on TV? Do you enjoy them?
2 Do you think the advice on survival shows is useful?
3 Imagine yourself in a dangerous situation like Jake's. Do you think you would survive?

Writing • Giving instructions

1 **Read the Writing File.**

> **Writing File** Giving clear instructions
>
> **Use headings so people can find the right information quickly.**
>
> - **Use bullet points.**
> - **Keep sentences short.**
> - **Don't use linking words at the beginning of sentences.**

2 **Read the information pamphlet. How many bullet points are there? How many sentences are there in the longest bullet points?**

HOW TO Survive an Earthquake

Be prepared

- If the danger of earthquakes is high in your area, find out about organizations that can send free earthquake warnings by text message. You might have a few seconds before the earthquake reaches you. A few seconds could save your life.

Before or during an earthquake

- People inside buildings should hide under a sturdy table or desk, away from windows and heavy objects on walls.
- If you are cooking, turn off the gas or electricity.
- People in outside areas should move away from buildings, trees and power lines.
- Drivers should drive carefully away from bridges, buildings, trees and power lines, and then stop their car. They shouldn't leave the car.

After an earthquake

- In areas near the ocean, tsunamis sometimes develop after earthquakes. You should listen to the radio. If there is any danger of a tsunami in your area, run to high ground.

3 **Match the headings (1–3) to the advice (a–c).**

1 Avoid the problem
2 Reduce the danger
3 During an attack

a Never swim in waters where there have been recent shark attacks.
b Hit the shark hard in the eyes or the end of its nose.
c Wear dark clothes. To a shark, people in bright colors might look like fish.

4 **You are going to write an information pamphlet about survival in the desert, or your own idea. Look at the ideas in the pictures and/or do your own research. Take some notes.**

5 **Write your information pamphlet. Use your notes from Exercise 4.**

> **Remember!**
> - Use headings and bullet points.
> - Use the vocabulary in this unit.
> - Check your grammar, spelling and punctuation.

Grammar • Review

1 Choose the correct options.

1 Rabbits *can't* / *must* fly.
2 You *could* / *mustn't* forget your book. You'll need it.
3 Last year I *must* / *had to* learn Chinese. It was really difficult.
4 I've been learning English for seven years, so I *can* / *have to* speak it pretty well now.
5 You *should* / *mustn't* try harder in class.
6 My mom *can't* / *couldn't* swim when she was a child.
7 You *mustn't* / *don't have to* wash your hair every day. Twice a week is enough.
8 We *had to* / *could* see the ocean from the house where we stayed last summer.
9 She *mustn't* / *should* forget her hockey stick today because she's playing in a game.
10 I *have to* / *can't* study tonight because we have an important test tomorrow.
11 You *can* / *shouldn't* swim in the lake. It's very dangerous.
12 My grandpa *mustn't* / *didn't have to* study science at school.

2 Complete the sentences with these verbs. Sometimes more than one answer is possible.

can't	could	might	must

1 He *must* like chocolate. Everyone likes chocolate!
2 She …. live in Costa Rica. I'm not sure.
3 I lost my bag. It …. be somewhere at school, or maybe at Tom's house.
4 He …. have a sister who's 30. His mom and dad are only 40.
5 They …. be from France. They don't speak any French.
6 The people near the erupting volcano …. feel very scared.
7 That car …. cost a lot of money. It's a BMW, and BMWs are always expensive.
8 She …. play the piano. I don't know.

Vocabulary • Review

3 Complete the sentences.

1 A *volcano* often produces ash when it e…. .
2 A…. happen in the mountains. If they b…. you in snow, it's very difficult to s…. .
3 If it doesn't rain for weeks, there's a d…. , and it can lead to a f…. . Many people s…. .
4 A h…. is a very strong wind that can d…. houses.
5 A serious d…. can s…. among people very quickly.
6 T…. are big waves after an e…. out in the ocean. They cause terrible f…. , and a lot of people d…. .

4 Complete the sentences with these words.

across	down (x2)	forward	of	off
on (x2)	out (x2)	through	to	

1 I came *across* Lia in town yesterday.
2 Put …. a sun hat. It'll protect you from sunburn.
3 We've run …. …. milk. I'll go and buy some more.
4 Calm …. . It's not the end of the world.
5 We're really looking …. …. our vacation.
6 She figured …. a way to cross the river safely.
7 I was late because our car broke …. .
8 Don't worry! You'll get …. the exams OK.
9 Take …. your sweater if you're too hot.
10 He kept …. walking until he found help.

Speaking • Review

5 Complete the conversation with these words. Then listen and check.
2.11

Are you saying	I don't understand.
I see!	~~What do you mean?~~

A We don't have to go to school tomorrow.
B [1] *What do you mean?* It's Monday tomorrow.
A Yes, but there's no school when there's a flood.
B Sorry, [2] …. [3] …. that there's a flood at school?
A Yes, there is. There's water in the classrooms.
B Oh, [4] …. Thanks for telling me.

Dictation

6 Listen and write in your notebook.
2.12

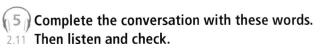

✓ **My assessment profile:** page 133

Richard Turere's Profile

Age	Home country
13	Kenya

My favorite things …

helping my family, inventing things

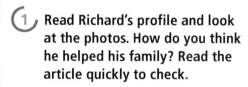

Reading

1 **Read Richard's profile and look at the photos. How do you think he helped his family? Read the article quickly to check.**

2 **Read the article again. Answer the questions.**
2.13

1 Why are lions a good thing for Kenya?
Because they attract hundreds of thousands of tourists every year.

2 Why do farmers kill them?

3 How many lions are there in Kenya?

4 Why couldn't Richard's farm have a fence to keep out the lions?

5 Why did his "lion lights" keep the lions away?

6 Was it expensive to make the lights?

7 What two groups did his lights help?

8 How has Richard's life changed since people heard about his lights?

Lion Lights

Lions are important to the people of Kenya because they attract hundreds of thousands of tourists every year. However, they also kill a lot of farm animals. In a country where droughts are common, it's hard for farmers to feed their families. It isn't surprising that they sometimes kill lions to protect their farms.

Twenty years ago, there were 10,000 lions in Kenya. Now there are only 2,000. Conservationists started to think that there was no hope for the lions' future. But then they heard about Richard Turere.

From the age of nine, it was Richard's job to take care of his family's cows. But when lions came out of the forest at night and ate them, Richard could do nothing. A fence high enough and strong enough to keep the lions out was too expensive.

When he was eleven, Richard realized that the lions never attacked when someone was moving around outside with a flashlight. They were afraid of humans. This gave Richard an idea. Maybe he could design some lights that could trick the lions. With an old car battery, a solar panel and some bulbs from broken flashlights, he created outside lights that looked like a moving flashlight. Since then, the lions have never come back to his farm.

Soon his neighbors asked him to put up "lion lights" at their farms, too. Again, the lights worked perfectly. Conservationists were very excited! Here was something simple and cheap that could both help farmers to feed their families and help the lions to survive.

And there was help for Richard, too. One of Kenya's best schools heard about his clever invention and offered him a free education there. Richard now hopes to become an engineer and invent many other useful things in the future.

Class discussion

1 What do you think is more important, the lions or the farmers' animals? Why?

2 Do you know of any other simple ideas to keep unwanted animals away?

3 What did you have to do when you were eleven? Compare your life at that age with Richard's life.

Grammar • Modals: ability, obligation, prohibition, advice

1 Complete the second sentence so that it means the same as the first. Use the verbs given. There may be more than one possible answer.

1 It's not necessary to wear a helmet when you ride a scooter.
   You *don't have to wear a helmet* when you ride a scooter.
2 I advise you to take some food to the party.
   You .... to the party.
3 It's a bad idea to forget your sister's birthday.
   You .... sister's birthday.
4 Leave your bags outside the classroom!
   You .... outside the classroom.
5 No talking in the library!
   We .... in the library.
6 She is able to play the guitar, but she isn't able to play the piano.
   She .... the guitar, but she .... the piano.

• Past modals

2 Put these sentences into the past tense.

1 Sarah can't read well without her glasses.
   Sarah couldn't read well without her glasses.
2 We have to take the dog for a walk.
3 They don't have to study over summer break.
4 I can hear you, but I can't see you.
5 They must be at the theater at 6 o'clock.

• Modals: possibility

3 Choose the correct options.

A Is this John's bag?
B No, it [1] *can't / could* be John's bag. John's bag is blue, and this one is red.
A Well, it [2] *must / could* be Henry's bag. His is red.
B Yes, it [3] *could / can't* be Henry's, or it [4] *might / must* be Jade's. Her bag is red, too.
A Let's look inside. Aha, this book has Jade's name in it.
B So it [5] *must / can't* be Jade's bag!

• Will/Going to

4 Choose the correct options.

1 A I'm hungry.
   B I*'m going to / 'll* make you a sandwich.
2 A What *are you going to / will you* do over the summer break?
   B We*'re going to / will* sail the ocean!
3 Oh no! It's 8 o'clock already. We*'re going to / will* miss the bus.
4 A Where do you think you *are going to / will* live in 2020?
   B I think I*'m going to / 'll* live on my own private island!
5 A *Are you going to / Will you* go to Amy's birthday party tonight?
   B Yes, I *am / will*. How about you?
   A No, I can't. But I've already sent her a card.

5 Complete the sentences with *will* or *going to* and the verbs in parentheses.

1 I think my team *will win* (win) the next game.
2 My friends and I .... (meet) at the movie theater tomorrow at 5 o'clock, but I don't know which movie we .... (see) yet.
3 A Oh no! The car's not working.
   B Don't worry. We .... (take) the bus to school.
4 I broke my brother's new cell phone.
   He .... (be) really angry with me!
5 What .... (study) in college next year?

• Present simple and Present continuous for future

6 Complete the text with the Present simple or Present continuous form of the verbs in parentheses.

I'm looking forward to tomorrow—I have a lot of plans. My singing lesson [1] *starts* (start) at 9 a.m., and it [2] .... (end) at 10:30 a.m. Then I [3] .... (meet) my friends in the park. In the afternoon, we [4] .... (take) a train to Philadelphia. The train [5] .... (leave) at 3:30 p.m. We [6] .... (visit) the Rodin Museum, and then we [7] .... (go) to the theater in the evening. What [8] .... (you/do) tomorrow?

Passive statements

7 **Make these sentences passive.**

1 People make chocolate from cacao beans.
   Chocolate *is made from cacao beans*.
2 They produce Sony computers in Japan.
   Sony computers .... .
3 They won't clean your windows tomorrow.
   Your windows .... .
4 Someone broke this plate yesterday.
   This plate .... .
5 Van Gogh didn't paint the *Mona Lisa*.
   The *Mona Lisa* .... .
6 People will discover new sources of energy
   in the future.
   New sources of energy .... .

8 **Complete the text with the correct passive form of the verbs in parentheses.**

In the past, most clothes [1] *were made* (make) out of natural materials like leather or cotton, and they [2] .... (sew) by hand at home. Now man-made materials like polyester [3] .... (use), and most clothes [4] .... (make) in factories. Who knows how our clothes [5] .... (produce) in the future? Perhaps new materials [6] .... (discover).

Passive questions

9 **Make these questions passive.**

1 Who makes this beautiful jewelry?
   Who is this beautiful jewelry made by?
2 When did they set up the company?
3 Does your teacher check your homework?
4 Will they decorate your room on Tuesday?
5 How did they find the shipwreck?

10 **Make passive questions for these answers. Use the question words.**

1 My bag is made of leather and metal. (What)
   What is your bag made of?
2 This house was built in 1910. (When)
3 The book will be published by Penguin Books. (Who)
4 The poem was written by Pablo Neruda. (Who)
5 These flowers are grown in Holland. (Where)

Speaking • Asking for clarification

1 **Put the conversation in the correct order.**

☐ a Oh, I see! Thanks.
☐ b Yes, I know. But all the streets are closed to traffic today.
[1] c We can't take the bus to the community center today.
☐ d No, the bike race is on the streets! But we can walk to the community center.
☐ e What do you mean? We always go by bus.
☐ f It's because of the bike race.
☐ g Are you saying that there's a bike race at the community center?
☐ h Sorry, I don't understand. Why are the streets closed?

Phone language

2 **Choose the correct options to complete the conversation.**

A Hello, Redhill Bookstore, can I help you?
B Hello, [1] *I'd like / I like* to speak to the manager, please.
A I'm sorry, he's talking to a customer at the moment. [2] *Can / Do* I take a message?
B Yes, please. My name's Emma Moore. I'm calling [3] *after / about* the salesperson job.
A Oh, the manager's free now. [4] *Hold / Wait* on, please. I'll [5] *transfer / put* you to him now.

Asking for and giving directions

3 **Complete the conversations with these phrases.**

can't miss	Cross	~~give me directions~~
Go past	how do I	on the right
the second turn	turn left	

A Excuse me, could you [1] *give me directions* to the library?
B Yes, of course. [2] .... the street next to the school. Then take [3] .... on the right. It's [4] .... .
A Thank you so much.

A Excuse me, [5] .... get to the park?
B [6] .... the bank, and then [7] .... . You [8] .... it.
A Thank you.

Vocabulary • Natural disasters

1 **Complete the words for natural disasters.**

1 ts*unam*i
2 f_m__e
3 dr___ht
4 e__t_qu__e
5 fl__d
6 a_a___ch_
7 h_r_____e
8 di_ea__

• Phrasal verbs 2

2 **Complete the sentences with these words.**

across	down (x2)	forward to
~~off~~	~~on~~	on
out (x2)	through	

1 It was very hot, so I took *off* my sweater and put *on* some sunscreen.
2 If your car breaks .... on the highway or runs .... of gas, you should call for roadside assistance.
3 If you stop panicking and calm .... , we will be able to get .... this situation without an accident.
4 I came .... an interesting article in the newspaper a few days ago.
5 Are you looking .... your vacation next week?
6 Let's keep .... trying to fix this engine—I'm sure we can figure .... what's wrong with it.

• Work collocations

3 **Choose the correct options.**

1 *answer* / *prepare* the phone
2 *make* / *take* an appointment
3 *check* / *work* at the front desk
4 *deal* / *make* some copies
5 *prepare* / *give* a spreadsheet
6 *attend* / *write* a report
7 *deal* / *attend* a meeting
8 *order* / *give* a presentation
9 *check* / *attend* emails
10 *take* / *answer* payments
11 *give* / *order* office supplies
12 *give* / *deal* with inquiries

• Job qualities

4 **Read the sentences (1–4) and then match two descriptions from the box to each name.**

excellent IT skills	experienced	good communicator
~~patient~~	practical	punctual
~~reliable~~	team player	

Jim: *patient, reliable*   **Dan:** .... , ...
Helen: .... , ...   **Kerry:** .... , ...

1 Jim doesn't get angry easily, and you can always trust him.
2 Helen is never late, and she can do useful things.
3 Dan is good at using a computer, and he likes working with other people.
4 Kerry has had this job for ten years, and she is good at talking to people.

• Coastal life

5 **Complete the words.**

1 You can buy presents for your friends in a s*ouveni*r shop.
2 A common coastal bird is a s__g_ll.
3 You can sit in a b___h c___r on the beach.
4 If you're hungry, you can buy a h_t d__ and then go to an i_e cr__m s__nd.
5 There is often an ar__d_ near the pi__.
6 Get some shade under a b__ch u_____la.

• Verbs with prefixes *dis-* and *re-*

6 **Match the verbs (a–h) to the definitions (1–8).**

1 think someone is wrong *b*
2 allow someone to leave a place
3 find something
4 take something away from somewhere
5 find out information about something
6 not like someone/something
7 get better
8 stop making something

a research
b disagree
c dislike
d remove

e release
f discover
g recover
h discontinue

Word list ⟳

Unit 4 • Survive!

Natural disasters

avalanche	/ˈævəˌlæntʃ/
bury	/ˈbɛri/
destroy	/dɪˈstrɔɪ/
disease	/dɪˈziz/
drought	/draʊt/
drown	/draʊn/
earthquake	/ˈɚθkweɪk/
erupt	/ɪˌrʌpt/
famine	/ˈfæmɪn/
flood	/flʌd/
hurricane	/ˈhɚɪˌkeɪn, ˈhʌr-/
spread	/sprɛd/
starve	/starv/
survive	/səˈvaɪv/
tsunami	/tsʊˈnami/
volcano	/vɑlˈkeɪnoʊ/

Phrasal verbs 2

break down	/ˌbreɪk ˈdaʊn/
calm down	/ˌkɑm ˈdaʊn/
come across	/ˌkʌm əˈkrɔs/
figure out	/ˌfɪɡyɚ ˈaʊt/
get through	/ˌɡɛt ˈθru/
keep on	/ˌkip ˈɔn/
look forward to	/ˌlʊk ˈfɔrwɚd tə/
put on	/ˈpʊt ˈɔn/
run out of	/ˌrʌn ˈaʊt əv/
take off	/ˌteɪk ˈɔf/

Unit 5 • Work for It

Work collocations

answer the phone	/ˈænsɚ ðə ˈfoʊn/
attend a meeting	/əˌtɛnd ə ˈmiʈ ɪŋ/
check emails	/ˌtʃɛk ˈimeɪlz/
deal with inquiries	/dil wɪð ɪnˈkwaɪəriz/
give a presentation	/ɡɪv ə prɛzənˈteɪʃən/
make an appointment	/ˌmeɪk ən əˈpɔɪntˀmənt/
make some copies	/ˌmeɪk səm ˈkɑpiz/
order office supplies	/ˌɔrdɚ ˈɔfɪs səˌplaɪz/
prepare a spreadsheet	/prɪˌpɛr ə ˈsprɛdʃit/

take payments	/ˌteɪk ˈpeɪmənts/
work at the front desk	/ˈwɚk ət ðə ˌfrʌnt ˈdɛsk/
write a report	/ˌraɪt ə rɪˈpɔrt/

Job qualities

accurate	/ˈækyərɪt/
analytical	/ˌænlˈɪʈ ɪkəl/
excellent IT skills	/ˈɛksələnt ˌaɪ ˈti ˌskɪlz/
experienced	/ɪkˈspɪriənst/
good communicator	/ˌɡʊd kəˈmyunəˌkeɪtɚ/
leadership qualities	/ˈlidɚˌʃɪp ˈkwɑləʈ iz/
organized	/ˈɔrgəˌnaɪzd/
patient	/ˈpeɪʃənt/
practical	/ˈpræktɪkəl/
punctual	/ˈpʌŋktʃuəl/
reliable	/rɪˈlaɪəbəl/
team player	/ˈtim ˌpleɪɚ/

Unit 6 • Coast

Coastal life

arcade	/arˈkeɪd/
beach chair	/ˈbitʃ tʃɛr/
beach umbrella	/ˈbitʃ ʌmˈbrɛlə/
cliffs	/klɪfs/
go-cart	/ˈɡoʊkart/
harbor	/ˈharbɚ/
hot dog stand	/ˈhat dɔɡ ˈstænd/
ice cream stand	/ˈaɪs krim ˈstænd/
pier	/pɪr/
seagull	/ˈsigʌl/
seawall	/ˈsiwɔl/
souvenir shop	/ˌsuvəˈnɪr ˈʃɑp/

Verbs with prefixes dis- and re-

disagree	/ˌdɪsəˈgri/
disappear	/ˌdɪsəˈpɪr/
discontinue	/ˌdɪskənˈtɪnyu/
discover	/dɪˈskʌvɚ/
dislike	/dɪsˈlaɪk/
recover	/rɪˈkʌvɚ/
release	/rɪˈlis/
remove	/rɪˈmuv/
replace	/rɪˈpleɪs/
research	/ˈrisɚtʃ, rɪˈsɚtʃ/
restore	/rɪˈstɔr/

Brain Trainers

Unit 1

1 Look at the pieces of paper. Find one transportation word and one building word. You have two minutes.

ee · o · sc · p · ra · sp · sk · at · b · d · y · er

2a Find eight compound nouns. You have one minute.

snowmobile

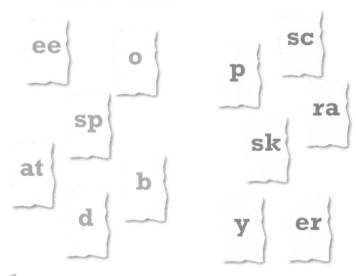

work · white · ~~snow~~ · home · wind · mill · house · ~~mobile~~ · baby · board · light · mate · class · person · sitter · business

2b Arrange the letters below to make a job word and a transportation word.

h · p · s · r · s · e · e · f · i · f · i · c · e · h · a · p · i · g · t · r

3 Work in pairs. Student A acts out a phrasal verb. Student B guesses the phrase. Switch roles.

find out · run away · get back · go out · set up · hang out · look for · give up · fill out · count on

Is it "get back"?

Unit 2

1 Choose a straight or diagonal line on the grid. Use the words and pictures to make up a story about something you want to do.

secret · crazy · ACTORS WANTED CALL NOW · dream come true

Brain Trainers

2 Look at the word webs for one minute. Cover them. Now write four phrases for each word web in your notebook.

a decision ← **make** → someone's dream come true

a difference   it to the finals

a secret ← **keep** → control

in touch   calm

crazy ← **go** → for a walk

together   well

3 Work in pairs. Identify a picture. Your partner identifies the matching word.

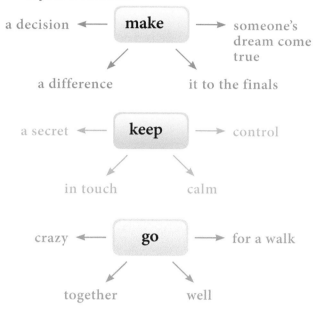

	1	2	3	4
A		poet		playwright
B		sculptor	art	
C		novelist	photographer	

A1 is a novel.

C2 is a novelist.

Unit 3

1a Look at the boy and girl. Can you find them in the crowd below? You have one minute.

1b Now work with a partner. Look at the crowd. Pick four people and take turns telling your partner how they are feeling.

2a How many feelings verbs can you think of with the letter *s*? Write them in your notebook.

2b Now can you think of these feelings verbs?

This is a three-letter word that ends in *y*.
This is a four-letter word. The third letter is *w*.
This is a five-letter word that begins with *f*.
This is a five-letter word that ends in *h*.

Brain Trainers

3 Look at the photos. Make adjectives from the nouns in the box to describe each photo.

| beauty | ~~danger~~ | fame | health | luck |
| peace | poison | success | wealth | |

1 *dangerous*

Unit 4

1 Look at the pieces of paper. Find two natural disaster words. You have two minutes.

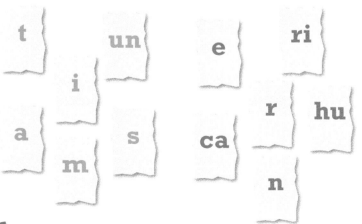

2 Work in pairs. Choose a noun from box 1. Your partner describes a natural disaster using a verb from box 2.

1	2
flood	starve
volcano	destroy
drought	erupt
famine	drown
avalanche	spread
disease	survive
earthquake	bury

flood

People can drown in a flood.

3a Work in pairs. Say a word from the list below. Your partner completes the phrasal verb. Write it in your notebook. Then switch roles. Check your answers.

take …	break …
keep …	**look forward …**
run …	figure …
calm …	**get …**
come …	put …

3b Now choose a phrasal verb from your list. Your partner makes a sentence using the phrasal verb. Switch roles.

Listening Bank

Unit 1

1 **Listen again. Choose the correct options.**

1.11
1. Laura was *11* / *15* when her life changed.
2. She was *going to school* / *going home*.
3. She was thinking about *music* / *homework*.
4. The band was playing *on the street* / *in the bookstore*.
5. She *loved* / *hated* the band's music.

2 **Listen again. Are these statements true (T) or false (F)?**

1.11
1. Laura is now a famous trumpet player. *T*
2. She was excited to hear the band because they were famous.
3. There were two trumpet players, a singer and a guitar player in the band.
4. After the band finished playing, she went home.
5. When Laura asked her mom for trumpet lessons, she immediately said yes.

Unit 2

1 **Listen again. Choose the correct options.**

1.24
1. Raj has *never* / *often* sung in public.
2. His rap is about *biology class* / *school lunches*.
3. *He* / *His sister* designed the burger costume for the video.
4. *He* / *His sister* plays the guitar and drums on the video.
5. Jennifer Marquez *posted a link to* / *wrote a review of* Raj's video on her blog.
6. *Jennifer Marquez* / *Larry Nixon* has invited Raj to come to New York.

2 **Listen again. Answer the questions.**

1.24
1. How old is Raj Patel? *14*
2. How many hits did his video get?
3. What does Raj do on the video?
4. Where will Raj perform the rap?
5. How does he feel about this?

Unit 3

1 **Listen again. Choose the correct options.**

1.35
1. Luke started *acting* / *being in movies* when he was five.
2. He was *glad* / *sad* when he didn't get a movie part.
3. Now he is *happy* / *sad* that he wasn't a famous child actor.
4. He thinks that famous child actors have a *crazy* / *amazing* kind of life.
5. It *is* / *isn't* easy for child stars to become successful actors as adults.
6. He *feels* / *doesn't feel* confident about his future.

2 **Listen again. Answer the questions.**

1.35
1. What did Luke do in school?
   He was in school plays.
2. Why is it hard for famous child actors to have normal friends?
3. What kind of people follow child actors?
4. Why is Luke famous now?
5. How old is he now?

Listening Bank

Unit 4

1 **Listen again. Choose the correct options.**

2.10
1 Mike thinks the participants in survival shows do *crazy* / *smart* things.
2 Some participants *eat things* / *interview people* that might give them a disease.
3 It *is* / *isn't* safe to swim across ice-cold rivers.
4 Mike talks about a man who *died* / *was rescued* last year.
5 It was *winter* / *summer* when this man was in the mountains.
6 Mike thinks that this person was *brave* / *stupid*.
7 In emergency situations, you *should* / *shouldn't* sleep in a snow cave.

2 **Listen again. Answer the questions.**

2.10
1 When is it OK to do the dangerous things seen on survival shows? *in an emergency*
2 What did the man in the mountains want to do?
3 What gave him this idea?
4 Why was he lucky?

Unit 5

1 **Listen again. Choose the correct options.**

2.23
1 Tom's training session starts in *10* / *30* minutes.
2 Tom is scared of *heights* / *flights*.
3 Tom is *usually* / *never* late.
4 Tom is picking up his costume *this afternoon* / *tomorrow*.
5 Anna is going to bring her *pirate costume* / *camera* when she visits the theme park.

2 **Listen again. Are these statements true (T)**
2.23 **or false (F)?**

1 Tom and Anna have arranged to meet at the theme park. *F*
2 Tom doesn't like theme parks.
3 Tom starts his job today.
4 Anna is surprised that Tom has a job at the theme park.
5 Anna doesn't think that Tom is good at working with other people.
6 Tom is going to wear unusual clothes for his job.
7 Anna takes a photo of Tom.

Unit 6

1 **Listen again. Put these events in the correct order.**

2.36
a It was used as a school for sailors.
b The *Cutty Sark* was built. *1*
c It was damaged in a fire.
d It came in second in a famous race.
e It was moved to Greenwich.

2 **Listen again. Complete the fact sheet.**
2.36

> CUTTY SARK FACT FILE
>
> 1 *Cutty Sark* was built in 1869 in *Scotland*.
> 2 It transported tea from .... to England.
> 3 In .... it was bought by Captain Dowman.
> 4 In .... it was moved to Greenwich and became a .... .
> 5 In 2007 it was badly damaged in a .... .
> 6 The repairs took five years to complete and cost over .... .
> 7 The ship is now raised .... meters above the ground.

Pronunciation

Unit 1 • Compound noun word stress

a **Listen and repeat. Then mark the stressed syllables.**
1.4

babysitter   firefighter   homework   speedboat

b **Listen, check your answers and repeat.**
1.4

Unit 2 • Sentence stress

a **Listen and repeat.**
1.18   1 Don't forget to keep in touch when you move.
2 I made a bad decision when I sold my bike.
3 Please try to keep control of your dog!

b **Listen again and find the stressed words.**
1.18

Unit 3 • Showing feelings

a **Listen and decide how each speaker is feeling.**
1.29 **Write *a* for speaker one or *b* for speaker two.**

1 What's that?   angry *b*   afraid *a*
2 It's great news!   excited ....   bored ....
3 Look! A shark!   afraid ....   excited ....

b **Listen again and repeat.**
1.29

Unit 4 • Consonant clusters

a **Listen and repeat.**
2.3   <u>spr</u>ead   eru<u>pt</u>   de<u>str</u>oy

b **Listen and repeat.**
2.4   1 The volcano erupted on Wednesday.
2 Don't scream so loudly! It's just a squirrel.
3 Stop spreading crazy stories.

Unit 5 • /ɚ/ and /ɔr/

a **Listen and repeat.**
2.15   /ɚ/ work   /ɔr/ report

b **Match these words to the correct sound**
2.16 **(/ɚ/ or /ɔr/). Then listen and check.**

bird   door   heard   order   serve   sport

Unit 6 • Weak vs strong form of *was*

a **Listen to the conversation. Underline the weak**
2.30 **pronunciation of *was* /wəz/.**

A **Was** there a beach festival here last year?
B Yes, there **was**. And a movie **was** made about it.
C It **was** directed by Felipe Trent.
B **Was** it really?
C Yes, it **was**. And it **was** shown on TV last night.

b **Listen again and repeat. Practice the conversation**
2.30 **in groups of three.**

Unit 7 • Elided syllables

a **Listen and repeat. How many syllables can you**
3.2 **hear in each word? Which letters aren't spoken?**

Wednesday   camera   comfortable

b **Listen and repeat. Find the letters that aren't**
3.3 **spoken in the underlined words.**

1 It's a <u>different</u> <u>temperature</u> today.
2 Do you prefer <u>chocolate</u> or <u>vegetables</u>?
3 They have some <u>interesting</u> <u>local</u> dishes here.

Unit 8 • /ɛr/, /i/ and /eɪ/

a **Listen and repeat.**
3.15   /ɛr/ wear   /i/ deal   /eɪ/ break

b **Match these words to the correct sound (/ɛr/, /i/**
3.16 **or /eɪ/). Then listen and check.**

air   chair   escape   heat   police   take

Unit 9 • /ʃ/, /ʒ/ and /dʒ/

a **Listen and repeat.**
3.27   /ʃ/ decorations   /ʒ/ casual   /dʒ/ jacket

b **Listen and repeat.**
3.28   1 She's studying geography in college.
2 I usually do martial arts in my pajamas.
3 The electrician left some trash in the garage.
4 He just watches action movies on television.

Reading

1 Read about Halloween. Name four countries
3.39 where Halloween is celebrated.

2 Read about Halloween again.
Answer the questions.

1 Why did people wear costumes on Halloween in the past?
2 Why do people sometimes throw eggs on Halloween?
3 Why do people put pumpkins outside their home?
4 Why is it lucky to find a ring in your cake on Halloween?

Your Culture

3 In pairs, answer the questions.

1 Do people in your country celebrate Halloween or All Saints' Day? What do they do?
2 Are there other festivals in which people wear costumes? Describe them.
3 Barmbrack has a ring inside it. Are there any traditions in your country in which people put objects or symbols inside food?

4 Write a short paragraph about Halloween in your country. Use your answers to Exercise 3 and the Halloween examples to help you.

HALLOWEEN

October 31 is Halloween, the night before All Saints' Day. In many parts of the world, it's the scariest night of the year!

Costumes in the past
People in Britain and Ireland used to believe that when people died, their souls stayed on earth until All Saints' Day. Halloween was the last time that these souls could get revenge on their enemies. For this reason, people wore costumes and masks so the souls couldn't recognize them.

Costumes today
Many people still wear costumes on Halloween today. In the UK, children usually dress as scary characters, like witches, zombies or vampires. In the US and Canada, a wider variety of costumes are worn, and there are a lot of costume parties for adults as well as children.

Trick-or-treaters
In their costumes, children go to people's homes and say "Trick or treat?" People usually give the children a treat—for example, some candy. If the children aren't given anything, they can sometimes play a trick on the people. For example, they might throw an egg at the front door.

Pumpkins
People cut a scary face into a pumpkin and light a candle inside it. They put this outside their house as a sign that they have treats for the trick-or-treaters.

Barmbrack
In Ireland, people eat a traditional fruitcake called "barmbrack" on Halloween. Inside the cake, there's a ring. The person with the ring in his or her piece of cake will find true love in the next year.

Reading

1 Read about New Year's Eve. Where do these
3.40 traditions come from?

> first-footing   a cake   beach parties
> a ball of lights   a song about old friends

2 Read about New Year's Eve again.
Answer the questions.

1 What is Hogmanay?
2 What happens on Sydney Harbor Bridge?
3 What do people do when they sing *Auld Lang Syne*?
4 What is a New Year's Resolution?

3 In pairs, answer the questions.

1 Do people in your country celebrate New Year's Eve? How?
2 Do they have special food or drink on that night?
3 *Auld Lang Syne* is a traditional song for New Year's Eve. What traditional songs are associated with festivals in your country?

4 Write a short paragraph about New Year's Eve in your country. Use your answers to Exercise 3 and the New Year's Eve examples to help you.

December 31

At midnight on December 31, we say goodbye to the old year and welcome the new one. Here are some of the traditions around the world.

Hogmanay
This is the Scottish word for New Year, and it's a very important celebration in Scotland. After midnight, people go "first-footing." This means being the first person of the year to enter someone else's home. It brings good luck to the household. First-footers are usually given food and drink, but they can also bring a cake as a gift for the homeowner and his or her family.

New Year on the beach
In Australia, New Year's Eve is in summer. Most Australians celebrate outside—on boats, in parks or at the beach. In Sydney, there is a parade of boats in the harbor, and at midnight, there is a spectacular fireworks display on Sydney Harbor Bridge.

Times Square
About a million people go to Times Square in New York on New Year's Eve. A big ball of lights drops slowly down a flagpole. When it reaches the bottom, the new year has begun!

Auld Lang Syne
This is a traditional Scottish song about remembering old friends. It is sung in many parts of the world at midnight on New Year's Eve. To sing the song, people stand in a circle, cross their arms and hold hands.

New Year's Resolutions
On New Year's Day, a lot of people decide to stop a bad habit or start a good one. This decision is called a "New Year's Resolution." More people exercise in January than in any other month. Unfortunately, most resolutions are forgotten by the beginning of February!

Reading

1 Read about Chinese New Year. Put these Chinese
3.41 New Year traditions in the correct order.

> a big meal   cleaning the house
> dragon dances   painting the house door red

2 Read about Chinese New Year again.
Answer the questions.

1 Why are Chinese New Year decorations often red?
2 How long is the vacation that people have
   at New Year in China?
3 Why are red envelopes important at New Year?
4 Why do people go to Chinatown in Sydney
   at Chinese New Year?

Your Culture

3 In pairs, answer the questions.

1 Are there any Chinese New Year celebrations
   in your country? What happens at them?
2 Are there any other important festivals from
   other cultures that are celebrated in your
   country? Which?
3 Fireworks are an important part of Chinese
   New Year. Do you have fireworks in your
   country? When?

4 Write a short paragraph about Chinese New Year
or another festival celebrated in your country.
Use your answers to Exercise 3 and the Chinese
New Year examples to help you.

CHINESE NEW YEAR

New Year is the longest and most
important festival in China, but it
isn't celebrated on January 1.
It is on a different date each year,
between January 21 and
February 20.

Preparations

The whole house is cleaned before
the festival to sweep away the bad
luck of the previous year. Red is
a lucky color in China, so people
often put up red decorations or
paint their doors red. The house is
now ready to welcome the good
luck of the New Year.

Reunion dinner

Many people in China live a long
way from their family, but everyone
can go home at New Year because
there are seven days of vacation.
On the night before New Year,
there is a special meal for the
whole family.

New Year's Day

There are fireworks to drive away
evil spirits. There are lion and
dragon dances, too. Parents and
grandparents give children money
in red envelopes.

Chinese New Year around
the world

Chinese New Year is an important
festival in every place where
large groups of Chinese people
are living. It is a public holiday in
Malaysia, Singapore, Mauritius,
Indonesia and the Philippines.
There are parades in many cities,
including San Francisco and Los
Angeles (US), London (UK), Toronto
(Canada) and Wellington (New
Zealand). The biggest celebration
outside Asia, however, is in Sydney
(Australia). More than 600,000 people
go to the city's Chinatown every
year to enjoy Chinese food,
parades, dragon boat races and
performances from some of Asia's
best singers and dancers.

|||MOVE IT!

WORKBOOK WITH MP3S

SPLIT EDITION

4A

BESS BRADFIELD

SERIES CONSULTANT: CARA NORRIS-RAMIREZ

Contents

Starter Unit

Grammar and Vocabulary

• *To be* and *have*

1 Write sentences and questions. Use the correct form of **be** or *have*.

1 My teacher / red hair ✗
   My teacher doesn't have red hair.
2 I / fifteen years old ✓
   ....
3 your friends / any interesting hobbies ?
   ....
   ....
4 Our house / a yard ✓
   ....
   ....
5 you / afraid / of anything ?
   ....
6 It / sunny today ✗
   ....
7 My parents / a blue car ✓
   ....
   ....
8 They / hungry ✗
   ....

• Daily routines

2 Match the verbs (1–9) to the phrases (a–i) to make daily routine collocations. Which of these things did you do yesterday?

1 walk   a to school by car
2 drive   b the bus
3 brush   c the dishes
4 do   d your bed
5 get on   e the dog
6 do   f a shower
7 take   g your homework
8 get   h dressed
9 make   i your teeth

• Present simple

3 Complete the conversations with the Present simple form of these verbs. Then complete the short answers.

| cook   do (x2)   go   ~~like~~   live   not clean   not like   play |

1 **A** *Do you and your friends like* (you and your friends) shopping?
   B No, we .... shopping—it's boring! We prefer video games.
2 **A** .... (you) basketball in your free time?
   B Yes, I .... I also .... judo.
3 **A** .... (your best friend) near you?
   B No, she .... ! She .... to school in the UK—5,000 kilometers away!
4 **A** .... (who) the housework in your home?
   B My dad always .... dinner, but he .... the house. I usually do that!

• Present continuous

4 Choose the correct options. Use the Present continuous forms to complete the email.

| New Message   ⊗ |

Hi Annie,   **Send**
¹ *Are you having* (you – *have* / *like*) a good weekend?
We ² .... (*do* / *have*) a great time at the campsite! Right now, my brother and my sister
³ .... (*play* / *do*) tennis. My dad ⁴
.... (*cook* / *make*) sausages and burgers on the grill, and my mom and I … well, we ⁵ ....
(*not do* / *not work*) anything! The sun ⁶ ....
(*not light* / *not shine*), but that's OK—it's still really hot!
What ⁷ .... (you – *do* / *make*) at the moment?
Love,
Lila x

• Present simple vs Present continuous

5 Complete the description of the photo. Use the Present simple or Present continuous form of the verbs. Then answer the question below.

This is a photo of my family. ¹ *Do you like* (you/like) it? In this photo, we ²........................ (smile)—we ³........................ (smile) a lot in my family. I'm Angela. I ⁴........................ (sit) in the middle, and my parents (Frank and Gaby) ⁵........................ (stand) behind me. I ⁶........................ (think) my smile is the biggest! In the photo, my dad (Frank) ⁷........................ (wear) a shirt. He ⁸........................ (usually/wear) T-shirts! My brother Reyes ⁹........................ (appear) on the right, near Mom. Javi is on the left.

Who are the people in the photo? Write the names.

A ....   D ....
B ....   E ....
C ....

• Apostrophes

6 Rewrite the text. Add apostrophes where necessary.

My uncles named Tom. Hes married to Tess, and they have six children! My cousin Jake has five sisters, but he doesnt have any brothers. Jakes sisters names are Lily, Gina, Jo, Ava and Meg. Theres also a dog, whos very friendly. Its names Lucky, and he loves long walks when its sunny.

My uncle's named Tom.........................
....
....
....
....
....

• Pronouns and possessive adjectives

7 Complete the sentences with the pronoun or possessive adjective that relates to the words in bold.

1 Is that **Dan**? What's *he* doing here?
2 Please hand this book to **John**. It isn't mine, it's ....
3 They're my **neighbors**. But I don't like .... very much!
4 **We** live here. This house is ....
5 "What's .... name?" "It's **Sophie**."
6 I think **this bag** belongs to **you**. Look, ... has .... name on it.

• Useful adjectives

8 Complete Eve's vacation journal with these adjectives.

colorful	dirty	disgusting	excellent	huge
~~lovely~~	popular	quiet	sore	tiny

Saturday

It's a ¹ lovely, cool evening in San Francisco. It's a ²........................ city—one of the biggest in the US! It's really ³........................ with tourists, too. I loved the ⁴........................ buildings in blue, green and yellow. My only criticism? My feet feel ⁵........................ after walking all day!

Monday

After the city noise, the Sierra National Forest seems ⁶........................ . We're staying in a ⁷........................ town, with just a few houses. The only café is ⁸........................ (it needs a cleaning!), and the food tastes ⁹........................ ! Dad says we're leaving tomorrow. I think that's an ¹⁰........................ idea.

• Comparatives and superlatives

9 Complete the questions. Use the comparative or superlative form of the adjectives. Then answer the questions.

1 Is your best friend *older than* you, or .... you? (~~old~~/young)
2 Who is .... person in your family? (funny)
3 What is .... place in your country? (beautiful)
4 Are movies .... books? (good)
5 What do you think is .... day of the week? (bad)
6 Is math .... English? (difficult)

• Free-time activities

10 Cross out the word that does *not* belong.

1 do *judo* / *track* / ~~the drums~~
2 listen to *reggae* / *classical* / *fantasy* music
3 watch a *horror* / *rap* / *comedy* movie
4 play *ice hockey* / *the saxophone* / *surfing*
5 go *gymnastics* / *swimming* / *skiing*

11 Complete the sentences with the Past simple forms of appropriate verbs.

On Sunday …
1 Jonah *sent* text messages, ... the drums and .... to rock music.
2 Nell .... basketball, ... gymnastics and .... fantasy movies.
3 Ali .... tennis, ... the Internet and .... the keyboard.

• Relative pronouns

12 Complete the definitions. Write **who, which** or **where** and add appropriate words.

1 Doctors and nurses are people *who* work in *hospitals*.
2 A teacher is a person .... works in a ....
3 A library is a place .... you can read a lot of ....
4 A pen is an object .... you use to .... with.
5 Snakes are long, thin animals .... don't have .... !

• Some and any

13 Write sentences and questions with *some* or *any*. Use the Present simple.

1 I / have / money with me ✗
I don't have any money with me.
2 There / be / orange juice in the fridge ✓
....
....
3 be / there / museums in your town ?
....
....
4 We / have / classes / on Saturdays ✗
....
....
5 My dad / usually / eats / cereal for breakfast ✓
....
....
6 he / like / interesting bands ?
....
7 I / usually / do / work / on Sundays ✗
....
....

• Much, many and a lot of

14 a Choose the correct options. Then answer the question below.

I have ¹a lot of / much posters on my bedroom walls. I have ²much / a lot of sports clothes, but I don't have ³many / much clean clothes at the moment! I have ⁴a lot of / much books, but I don't spend ⁵much / many time reading them! I don't have ⁶much / many comics. I like them, but reading comics isn't my favorite hobby. I have a guitar, but I don't know ⁷many / much songs yet. I don't have any drums (my favorite instrument)—Dad says they make too ⁸many / much noise! Mom says there's too ⁹many / much mess in my room, but I think it's perfect …

b **Compare the picture of Caleb's bedroom with the text. Can you find a mistake in the picture?**

• Feelings adjectives

(15) **Put the letters in the correct order to complete feelings adjectives. Which adjectives are positive (🙂)?**

1 t*ired*   (ider)
2 a.......................   (nryg)
3 u.......................   (tsep)
4 b.......................   (erod)
5 p.......................   (odur)
6 lo.......................   (lyne)
7 af.......................   (idra)
8 ex.......................   (itcde)
9 ne.......................   (ovurs)
10 je.......................   (sloua)
11 re.......................   (axeld)
12 em.......................   (edbssarar)

• Past simple

(16) **Complete the text. Use the Past simple affirmative, negative or question form of *be.***

I remember a time when I ¹ *was* two. It ².....................
my twin sisters' birthday party. They ³.......................
four that day! There ⁴....................... a lot of
presents, but they ⁵....................... for me.
I ⁶....................... very happy. I think I cried! What's
your earliest memory? ⁷.......................(it) a happy
or a sad time? How old ⁸.......................(you)?

(17) **Rewrite the sentences and questions in the Past simple.**

1 I watch TV and study.
   I watched TV and studied.
2 I don't walk to school.
   ....
3 Do you play the violin? Yes, I do.
   .... ?
   ....
4 He likes Dana, so he carries her books.
   ....
5 Max doesn't talk much because he's shy.
   ....
6 Does Mr. Scott live here? No, he doesn't.
   .... ?
   ....

• Irregular verbs

(18) **Complete the text. Use the Past simple form of the verbs.**

I ¹*got* (get) up very late on Saturday.
Then I ².......................(eat) a huge
breakfast and ³.......................(drink)
some coffee. Later, I ⁴.......................(go)
to the mall, and I ⁵.......................(buy) a
new video game. Jamie ⁶.......................
(come) over in the afternoon, and we
played for a while. He's really good,
so I ⁷.......................(lose)! After dinner,
I ⁸.......................(write) a few emails,
and I ⁹.......................(send) some photos
to a friend. Oh, yes, and I ¹⁰.......................
(do) a little homework, too! What did you
do last Saturday?

• Telling the time

(19) **Write the time in words.**

1 `1:45`   *a quarter to two*
2 `9:00`   ....
3 `3:10`   ....
4 `7:45`   ....
5 `3:55`   ....
6 `11:30` ....

① Different Lives

Vocabulary • Compound nouns

★ 1 Match (1–8) to (a–h) to make compound nouns. Then match them to the pictures.

1 business   a board
2 white   b boat
3 snow   c sitter
4 space   d person   *Picture 6*
5 baby   e ship
6 wind   f mill
7 speed   g work
8 home   h mobile

★★ 2 Complete the compound nouns in the box. Then use these words to complete the sentences.

business p _ _ _ _ n	class _ _ _ e	homew _ _ k
skyscr _ _ _ r	~~speedb o a t~~	wind _ _ _ l

1 The world's fastest *speedboat* traveled over the water at a speed of 511 km/h!
2 According to my ...., our math teacher is planning a surprise test!
3 I'm sure my English .... is getting easier and easier!
4 I was born near a big .... in the country. Now I live in an apartment in a .... in the city.
5 My mom is a .... She's ambitious and wants to start her own company.

★★ 3 Complete the text with compound nouns. Match a word from list A to a word from list B.

A	~~class~~	class	home
	light	speed	white

B	board	boats	house
	mates	~~room~~	work

It's ten o'clock, and I'm sitting in a ¹*classroom* in school. The teacher is writing the answers to last night's ²......................... on the ³......................... . I'm looking out the window, where I can see the ocean. There are some small, but fast and noisy ⁴......................... on the water. There's a tall, white ⁵......................... on the cliff that warns ships about the dangerous rocks below. It looks like a beautiful day. I wish my ⁶......................... and I could go outside!

★★ 4 Complete the definitions with compound nouns. Use the singular or plural forms.

1 A w*indmill* is a tall building that uses wind power for energy.
2 A f......................... is a person who prevents buildings from burning down.
3 S......................... are small vehicles that people use to travel across snow.
4 A s......................... is a vehicle that travels in space.
5 A l......................... is a tall building that shines a light out across the ocean to warn ships of dangerous rocks.
6 A b......................... is a person who takes care of children while their parents are out.

Workbook page 118

Reading

Brain Trainer

Always read a text at least twice!
Read quickly the first time to understand
the main ideas.
Do not stop reading when you see difficult
words or sentences.

Now do Exercise 1.

★ **1** Read the diary quickly. Complete the summary with the correct options.

Sophie is from ¹ *the US / Australia.*
She is writing about her experiences
of ² *moving to / taking a vacation in*
³ *the US / Australia.*

★ **2** How do Sophie's feelings about her experiences change? Choose the best diagram.

A 😠 → 🙂 → 🙁
B 🙂 → 😐 → 🙁
C 🙂 → 🙁 → 🙂

★★ **3** Read the diary again and find these numbers in the text. They may appear in a different order. Complete the sentences.

1 *5* – There are five *classrooms* in the school.
2 *8,000,000* – There are around 8,000,000 ....
   in ....
3 *2* – Sophie saw two ....
4 *389* – There are 389 .... in Sophie's
   ....
5 *45* – .... are forty-five.
6 *15* – There are fifteen .... in the
   ....

★★ **4** Are the statements true (T) or false (F)? <u>Underline</u> the evidence for your answers in the text.

1 Sophie's last home was small.   F
2 More people live in Tokyo than in New York.   ....
3 Sophie wasn't happy when her parents
  got a motorcycle.   ....
4 All the students at Sophie's new school are friendly. ....
5 Sophie feels upset about her first day at school.   ....
6 The only way Sophie can get to school is on foot.   ....
7 Sophie stepped on an insect by mistake.   ....
8 Sophie still doesn't like everything about her new home. ....

A NEW LIFE DOWN UNDER
by SOPHIE HICKS

DAY 1

We came straight from the airport to the farmhouse.
It's *huge*! <u>Our old apartment was the opposite of small</u>, but
now we have fifteen rooms, including a sports room with a
foosball table! Amazing.

DAY 2

This time last week, I was living in one of the world's biggest
cities. More than 8,000,000 people live in New York, almost
as many as in Tokyo. My new town has a population of 389!
I miss people, skyscrapers and traffic! We don't even have
a car here.

DAY 4

We now have a vehicle. But this isn't good news. When I went
outside this morning, Dad and Mom were riding around the
farm on an old motorcycle! They were laughing like teenagers.
They're *forty-five.*

Posted March 9 by Sophie Hicks

DAY 7

There are only five classrooms in my new school (and a
windmill to power the electricity)! I was really nervous at
first, but all my classmates were very nice. Well, apart from
one boy who laughed at my English pronunciation, but I
didn't mind too much. There's always one school idiot!

DAY 10

This morning, Dad offered me a ride to school on the
motorcycle, but I was too embarrassed. That was a mistake.
While I was walking, I saw two scorpions, and I almost
stepped on a big, black tarantula! In the US, there were flies
and sometimes a few *little* spiders. Australian insects belong
in horror movies!

DAY 15

Maybe this move isn't so bad. Yes, it's quiet, the animals are
scary, and I'm still not sure about the motorcycle. But people
are really friendly, and it's hard to be sad when it's sunny
every day!

Grammar • Past simple vs Past continuous

★ **1** Look at the photo. Complete the sentences with the Past simple or Past continuous form of the verbs.

Past continuous

1 At the time of the crash, Carl *was going* (go) to work.
2 He .... (drink) coffee.
3 He .... (send) a text.
4 He .... (not look) at the road.

Past simple

5 Carl .... (not see) the stop sign.
6 Luckily, he .... (get) better quickly after the accident!
7 He never .... (use) his phone again while he was driving.

★ **2** Choose the correct options.

1 **A** *Did you have* / *Were you having* a good summer vacation?
  B It was wonderful, thanks. This time last week I was on the beach. I *didn't sit* / *wasn't sitting* in a classroom!
2 **A** Oh no! What *happened* / *was happening* to you?
  B I broke my leg while I *rode* / *was riding* a snowmobile!
3 **A** What *did you do* / *were you doing* when I called at nine o'clock last night?
  B Sorry. I *didn't hear* / *wasn't hearing* the phone. I was doing my homework!

★ **3** Underline *while* and *when* in the sentences. Complete the sentences with the Past simple or the Past continuous form of the verbs.

1 <u>While</u> I *was walking* (walk) home one day, I *met* (meet) a man who changed my life.
2 When I .... (be) born, my parents .... (live) in a farmhouse.
3 I .... (lost) my passport while I .... (run) through the airport.
4 I .... (swim) in the ocean when I .... (see) Max on a speedboat.
5 The light in the lighthouse .... (not work) when the accident .... (happen).

★★ **4** Complete the text with the Past simple or Past continuous form of the verbs.

From the Streets to the Stadium

At this time yesterday, the Brazilian women's soccer team [1] *was playing* (play) in the Homeless World Cup. In the last ten minutes, Luana [2] .... (score) the winning goal! When Luana [3] .... (get) home to her apartment afterward, all her friends [4] .... (wait) for her. There was a big party!

But this time last year, Luana [5] .... (not live) in an apartment. She [6] .... (not have) a home at all. While Luana [7] .... (look) for a place to sleep one night, a friend [8] .... (tell) her about the Homeless World Cup. At that time, Brazilian members of the Homeless World Cup charity [9] .... (try) to help homeless people like Luana by building their confidence through sports.

Luana [10] .... (become) more confident while she [11] .... (learn) new skills. With the charity's help, she [12] .... (win) a scholarship to go to college.

Grammar Reference pages 110–111

Vocabulary • Phrasal verbs 1

Brain Trainer

Don't just write lists of new words in your vocabulary notebook. Write example sentences too, to help you remember how to use the words.

Do Exercise 1. Then write the example sentences for each phrasal verb in your notebook.

★ 1 **Match the sentence beginnings (1–8) to the endings (a–h).**

1 My dog ran   *d*
2 Could I borrow your pen to fill
3 I feel like Chinese food. Would you look
4 Come in and do some work! Don't hang
5 I'll call you after school. When do you usually get
6 We needed extra money, so we set
7 Don't stop trying! Don't give
8 If you don't understand what a word means, find

a out this form?
b back home in the afternoon?
c up just because something's a little difficult!
d away, and we never found her again.
e out by using a dictionary.
f out with your friends, doing nothing.
g up our own business.
h for a restaurant online?

★ 2 **Choose the correct options.**

1 Please .... your information here.
   (a) fill out   b find out   c set up
2 I'm .... my brother. Have you seen him?
   a giving up   b hanging out   c looking for
3 They .... a new charity.
   a set up   b ran away   c filled out
4 I .... that her name was Helen.
   a got, back   b found out   c gave up
5 He .... , and now we can't find him!
   a ran away   b filled out   c set up
6 We .... in town all day.
   a found out   b hung out   c counted on
7 I can't do this. I .... .
   a give up   b get back   c run away
8 I missed the last bus, so I .... late.
   a set up   b counted on   c got back

★ 3 **Complete the text with the correct form of these phrasal verbs.**

fill out	find out	get back	give up
~~go out~~	hang out	run away	set up

Yesterday was awful! I wanted to ¹*go out*, but I had to take care of my little brother while my parents were out. My aunt and uncle ² .... their anniversary party, and my parents went to help them decorate. I had some homework to do. While I ³ .... the answers, Harry got bored. At first he ⁴ .... in my room. I told him to go away. So he did. He went downstairs, opened the door—and ⁵ .... ! I looked for him everywhere. I didn't ⁶ .... ; I kept looking. Eventually, a neighbor called, and I ⁷ .... he was playing with a friend! We ⁸ .... home just before my parents did. I didn't tell them!

★ 4 **Look at the photos. Use the correct affirmative or negative form of the phrasal verbs from Exercise 3 to complete the sentences.**

1 *Please don't hang out* here.

2 .... this form.

3 Don't let the cat .... I'm taking it to the vet.

4 .... You can do it!

Workbook page 118

Speaking and Listening

★ (1) Match the questions (1–6) to the
2 answers (a–f). Then choose the correct
options. Listen and check your answers.

1 So, is your new school better than
the old one?   *f*
2 What's your favorite subject?
3 Do you do any after-school activities?
4 Do you like your new uniform?
5 What do you think of the school
cafeteria?
6 Is there anything else you don't like?

a I miss my old friends. They're *so /
such* far away!
b It's good! We used to have *so / really*
horrible food at my last school!
c No! It's brown. It's *such / so* an ugly
color. It's *such / really* awful!
d I'm in the skateboarding club.
It's *so / such* cool!
e English. We have a *really / such*
nice teacher. But I don't like math.
It's *so / such* a difficult subject!
f I don't think ⓢ*o* / *really*! But it's
different.

★ (2) Listen to a conversation. Complete the
3 answers with one word in each blank.

1 When did Anna move into her
new home?
A *month* ago.
2 Did Anna live in a bigger or smaller
city before?
A .... city.
3 What's the weather like where Anna
is today?
It's ....
4 What can Anna see from her window?
The ....
5 Which person in Anna's family
doesn't have a balcony?
Her ....
6 What is Anna sending Jake?
A ....

★★ (3) Listen again. What did Anna and Jake say about these
3 things? Complete the sentences with *really, so* or *such*
and these words or phrases.

a big city	a mess	a nice
beautiful views	cool house	disappointing
friendly	quiet	sister

1 New Orleans, Louisiana: *It's such a big city.*
2 The small town of Hamden: It's
....
3 Anna's new home: It's a ....
4 The worst thing about Anna's room:
It's ....
5 The best thing about Anna's room:
It has ....
6 The local people: They're ....
7 The weather: It's ....
8 Anna (according to Jake!):
You're ....

★★ (4) Choose *one* of the photos below. Imagine you moved to
this place last month! Write a conversation with a friend
back home. Use *really, so* and *such* at least once. Talk
about these things or use your own ideas.

| the people | the place | the weather | your new home |

Speaking and Listening page 122

Grammar • Used to

★ (1) **Complete the sentences. Use the affirmative or negative form of *used to*.**

1 This village *used to* be tiny, but then it grew!
2 I .... see fields out of my window. Now I see houses!
3 We .... have a lot to do here, but now we have a gym.
4 My friend Ben .... live here. His family moved here a few years ago.
5 I .... take the bus to school, because there wasn't a bus stop!
6 Sometimes I .... feel a little bored here, but now I like it a lot.

★ (2) **Complete the questions about life 200 years ago. Use the correct form of *used to* and a verb from the box. Then complete the answers.**

have	~~ride~~	travel
visit	work	

1 *Did* people *use to ride* snowmobiles?
   No, they didn't.
2 .... people .... on steamboats?
   .... , they did.
3 .... children .... in factories?
   Yes, they ....
4 .... schools .... whiteboards?
   No, ... didn't.
5 .... spaceships .... planet Earth?
   .... , they didn't.
   (We think!)

★★ (3) **Look at the photo. Write sentences about life in New York in 1900. Use the correct form of *used to* and these verbs.**

~~be~~	chat	drive
ride	take	wear

1 There / horses in New York
   There used to be horses in New York.
2 Most men / hats
   ....
   ....
   ....
3 Taxis / down the streets
   ....
   ....
   ....
4 People / on cell phones
   ....
5 Some people / bicycles
   ....
6 Cameras / color photographs
   ....

★★ (4) **Write questions with the correct form of *used to*. Then answer them so that they're true for you. Use the correct short form.**

Your life at age six

1 you and your family / in a city?   (live)
   Did you and your family use to live in a city?
   Yes, we did./No, we didn't.
2 you / vegetables?   (like)
   .... ?
   ....
3 you / to school / by yourself?   (walk)
   .... ?
   ....
4 you / cartoons?   (watch)
   .... ?
   ....
5 you and your family / a dog?   (have)
   .... ?
   ....
6 your bedroom / the same color?   (be)
   .... ?
   ....

Grammar Reference pages 110–111

Reading

1 **Read the article quickly. What is the main purpose of the text? Choose one option.**

 a to warn people about road safety
 b to tell an amazing personal story
 c to give a history of the Paralympics
 d to describe wheelchair basketball

LIFESTYLES

The Day That Changed Everything

"The day before yesterday," says Josh Peters, 16, "was probably the best day of my life." On that day, Josh found out that the national basketball team wanted him to play in the Paralympics!

Amazingly, two years ago, Josh didn't use to like any sports. "I was so lazy," says Josh. "The only exercise I did outside of school was going to the store to buy video games!"

On the day before his fourteenth birthday, Josh was crossing the street when a motorcycle hit him. The motorcyclist was riding so fast that he didn't see the red light—or Josh. Josh never walked again.

At first, Josh thought his life was over. "I didn't hang out with friends. I didn't answer their calls or emails. I just wanted to be alone." Then one day he saw a YouTube video about wheelchair basketball. "It looked so exciting," said Josh. "I wasn't watching 'people in wheelchairs.' I was watching great athletes!"

Josh joined a wheelchair basketball team in Colorado Springs. "My family lives in the city now, but we didn't then," explains Josh, "so I took a bus from my town every weekend to attend practice sessions. Friends often came with me. I realized how lucky I was to have such great friends."

Josh wasn't good at wheelchair basketball right away. "I fell over a lot, and I felt like such an idiot. I used to play 'ordinary' basketball at school, but that's easy. Compared to wheelchair basketball, it's slow!" However, Josh didn't give up, and he quickly impressed his coach, Andy Martin. "Josh's talent and determination are amazing. He's a Paralympian already."

How does Josh feel about his accident now? "Differently. Yes, it changed me. In a good way! Before it happened, I was just an average teenager. Now I'm competing for my country."

---

2 **Read the article again. Complete the sentences. Write one or two words in each blank.**

 1 Josh got some great news *two* days ago.
 2 Two years ago, Josh only used to play .... in his free time.
 3 Josh's accident happened when he was .... years old.
 4 The accident happened because .... didn't stop at a red light.
 5 Josh found out about wheelchair basketball when he watched a ....
 6 Josh mainly feels .... that his life changed.

Listening

1 **Listen to a radio show. What inspired the two main speakers? Choose *one* idea for each person.**
4

> a book   a movie   a song
> a TV show

 1 Rosa: ....
 2 Ali: ....

2 **Listen again. For each answer, write *Rosa, Ali* or *Rosa and Ali*.**
4

Who …
 1 found out what job they wanted to do?   *Ali*
 2 developed a completely new interest?   ....
 3 experienced a change on their birthday?   ....
 4 made a parent unhappy?
 ....
 5 felt inspired when a friend introduced him/her to something?
 ....
 6 used to get better grades in school?
 ....

Writing • Telling a story

1 Read the story quickly and put the paragraphs in order.

1 ....   2 ....   3 ....

A Birthday Surprise

A After an amazing dinner and *a lot* of cake, Dad set up the stereo in the backyard, and we chatted and danced till late. It was a really memorable night. My family and friends are so great. I [1] *'m* (be) very lucky!

B When school finished, I was feeling pretty sad. Then, while I [2] .... (walk) home, it started to rain. I really [3] .... (not have) a good day! By the time I got home, I just wanted to play video games and forget about everything. So I was so shocked when I [4] .... (open) the door—and saw all my family and friends! Everyone was shouting "surprise!"

C I always used to love birthdays, but this year was different. My family [5] .... (give) me a few cards at breakfast, and then I went to school. No one in my class remembered it was my birthday. I suggested going to the movies that night, but everyone said "Sorry, I [6] .... (be) busy."

---

2 Read the story in Exercise 1 again. Complete the text with the correct form of the verbs. Use the Present simple, Past simple or Past continuous.

3 a Complete the sentences. Use the Present simple, Past simple or Past continuous form of these verbs.

know	leave	live	open	put	~~walk~~

1 When I *walked* into the classroom, I was feeling really nervous.
2 I .... in a small town now, but last year I lived in a city skyscraper.
3 Marco .... the ring on Anna's finger when I sneezed! I was so embarrassed.
4 "....................... (you) what time it is?" the new boy asked me.
5 While everyone .... their presents, I took a family photo.
6 When she .... the hospital, she was crying loudly!

b Match the sentences (1–6) in Exercise 3a to the story headings (a–f) below.

a The first time I met my best friend   *4*
b My brother's/sister's wedding
c A special family celebration
d My first day at school
e A new baby in the family
f The day we moved to a new house

4 You are going to write a story about a memorable day in your own life. Choose an idea from Exercise 3, or your own idea. Then write notes in the paragraph plan below.

Paragraph 1: the background of the story ....
....

Paragraph 2: the main event ....
....

Paragraph 3: conclusion (what happened afterward and how you felt) ....
....

5 Write your story. Use the plan from Exercise 4 and include a mix of tenses.

....
....
....
....
....

Aiming High

Vocabulary • Collocations with *make*, *go* and *keep*

Brain Trainer

It is a good idea to record words that go together (collocations). This helps you to use language correctly.

make	go	keep
	well	

Now do Exercise 1.

★ **1** **Match the sentence beginnings (1–8) to the endings (a–h).**

1 How delicious! Waffles and fruit go   c
2 She moved to the US, but we kept
3 I studied every day. It really made
4 It's a nice day. Let's go
5 Relax! Keep
6 I thought my interview went
7 Yesterday the team made
8 Listen. Can you keep

a calm and try not to worry.
b well, but I didn't get the job.
c together perfectly!
d a secret?
e for a walk in the park.
f a difference in my final exam.
g it to the finals.
h in touch by videophone.

★ **2** **Choose the correct options.**

When I ¹(made)/ went / kept it to the finals of the judo tournament, it ² made / went / kept my dreams come true. On the day of the final round, I was really nervous, so I ³ made / went / kept for a walk. That ⁴ made / went / kept a difference because it helped me to ⁵ make / go / keep calm. But I didn't take my cell phone, so I didn't ⁶ make / go / keep in touch with my mom. That was a mistake. She ⁷ made / went / kept crazy with worry! Luckily, after I won the tournament and got back home, she forgave me.

★★ **3** **Complete the *make*, *go* and *keep* collocations in the text. Write one word in each blank.**

In 2009 an ordinary, 48-year-old woman surprised the world with her beautiful singing on *Britain's Got Talent*. Fans ¹ went crazy when Susan Boyle made ²........................ to the finals. The judges found it difficult to ³........................ control!

In the finals, a dance group won first prize, but fans of the show still made Susan's dreams come ⁴........................ . Her first album was number one around the world!

Fame quickly made ⁵........................ big difference in Susan's life. She became rich and performed in many different countries, including the US and Australia. But she says she still enjoys "ordinary" hobbies. She goes ⁶........................ walks, meets friends—and she loves spending time with her cat!

★★ **4** **Write the sentences or phrases. Use the correct form of *make*, *go* or *keep*.**

1 *Josh can't keep secrets.* (*Josh / can't / secrets*) He always tells someone.
2 .... (*Mom / crazy*) when I'm late for dinner!
3 .... (*Tom / in touch*) after he moved to Canada.
4 .... (*My parents / a big difference*) in my life when they bought me a laptop.
5 .... (*Marie / always / calm*) when I start worrying.
6 .... (*My dad / the decision*) to paint the house pink. It wasn't Mom's idea!
7 .... (*We / for a walk*) right now. Are you coming with us?

Workbook page 119

Reading

★ **1** **Read the webpage quickly. Then complete the title.**

How to M.........................
All Your D ....
C ....
T ....

★ **2** **What kind of writing is the webpage? Choose the correct option.**

a a factual report
b an informal article
c a formal essay
d an advertisement

★★ **3** **Read the webpage again. Match the headings (a–f) to the blanks (1–5). There is one heading you do not need.**

a Learn to love your mistakes
b Work hard
c How I can help you
d How to get rich
e Be yourself
f Have clear aims

★★ **4** **a** **Read the statements (1–7). According to the writer of the webpage, are the statements true (T), false (F) or don't know (DK)?**

1 Everyone has dreams
for the future.   *T*
2 Achieving your dreams
can be difficult.   ....
3 It's best to start with
a large, general aim.   ....
4 Life is easy when
you're famous.   ....
5 Successful people
don't make mistakes.   ....
6 Happiness is the most
important thing in life.   ....
7 Being successful means
being rich.   ....

b **Look at the statements in Exercise 4a again. What do you think?**

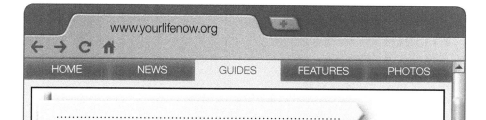

www.yourlifenow.org

HOME   NEWS   GUIDES   FEATURES   PHOTOS

....

1 ....

Have you ever had any dreams for the future? Yes, of course you have! But making your dreams come true isn't always easy. For the last ten years I've studied the lives of successful men and women, and my research has changed my life. But I don't want to keep my discoveries secret. Now let me share my best ideas with YOU!

2 ....

A lot of people think "I want to be rich/successful/famous," but these aims aren't helpful. They're too big! Instead, make a decision about exactly what you want to achieve in life and why. For example: "I've always loved writing. I want to study literature in college and then find work in the media."

3 ....

Have you ever noticed how busy celebrities are? Yes, they go to a lot of parties, but they don't often sit down and relax. They're always planning their next book, or movie or media interview. In reality, very few successful people are lazy. Sorry about that!

4 .*a*.

If you've never failed in life, you aren't human! If you get a bad grade, lose a competition or argue with your friends, keep calm. Think about what just happened. Can you do anything differently the next time? Failure is an excellent teacher.

5 ....

Finally, your biggest aim is to be happy! It's a good idea to listen to advice from parents or teachers, but remember that it's your life, and your dreams. What does "success" mean to you? Does it mean having a lot of money, or being close to family and friends? You decide.

HOW TO GUIDE no. 58

Do You   have a   dream?
?   ?
?   ?

Grammar • Present perfect

★ **1** **Choose the correct options.**

1 We've (already) / ever / yet entered the contest.
2 Has the team ever / yet / already made it to the finals before? No. This is their first time!
3 Why are you smiling? Have you already / yet / ever heard my amazing news?
4 I've yet / ever / never won any competitions before. This is a new experience for me.
5 Have you done your homework already / ever / yet? Yes. I've finished it!
6 She's never / already / yet made it to the finals. She's very talented.
7 I've ever / yet / never been on a motorcycle. It looks dangerous!
8 I haven't been to Greece yet / already / never, but I'd like to go there one day.

★ **2** **Complete the sentences with _for_ or _since_. Which sentences are true for you?**

1 I haven't eaten anything _since_ breakfast.
2 I've studied English .... more than ten years.
3 I've known my best friend .... elementary school.
4 I haven't listened to any music .... I got up.
5 I've lived in the same place .... my whole life.
6 I've had my own bedroom .... I was little.
7 I haven't watched any TV .... last night.
8 I haven't been to the movies .... more than a month.

★★ **3** **Complete the text with these words. Then answer the question below.**

| already | ~~ever~~ | for | never | since | yet |

The Woodford School's basketball team has won the finals!
Maria is organizing a party to celebrate.
Have you [1] _ever_ organized a party before? Who did you invite?
• Maria has invited Jake, but she hasn't talked to Layla [2] ....
• Ellie hasn't kept in touch with anyone [3] .... she moved.
• Matt has [4] .... been to a school party before, so he was excited to get an invitation.
• No one has seen Hasan [5] .... a week. He's been on vacation with his parents.
• Ed has [6] .... arranged to meet Layla at the party. He called her a while ago.

Who doesn't know about the party yet?
.... and ....

★★ **4** **Complete the conversations. Use the Present perfect with _already_, _ever_, _never_ or _yet_.**

1 A Why are they so happy?
  B Because _their favorite team has already won_! (their favorite team / win)
2 A Have you ever visited Europe?
  B No. .... !
    I prefer vacations at home. (I / go there)
3 A Do you want to watch _Avatar_?
  B No, thanks. ....
    We saw it a few years ago. (we / see / it)
4 A Please can I go out?
  B No, sorry! .... !
    (you / not finish / dinner)
5 A I haven't heard from Tess for ages. How's she doing?
  B No idea! I texted her a week ago, but ....
    (she / not reply)
6 A I can't decide where to go on vacation this year.
  B .... to Mexico? It's my favorite country.
    (you / go)

Grammar Reference pages 112–113

Vocabulary • Jobs and suffixes -or, -er, -ist

★ **(1)** **Complete the table with the jobs. Write the letters in the correct order.**

art form or object	person (job)
building	1 *builder* (ldiurbe)
poem	2 .... (tpeo)
novel	3 .... (nliovets)
play	4 .... (wrayhtplig)
art	5 .... (ratsit)
sculpture	6 .... (ostulprc)
photo	7 .... (grpotohhreap)

★ **(2)** **Complete the words in these definitions. Decide if each word refers to a *thing* or a *person*.**

1 An art*ist* paints or draws.
2 A doct.......... helps sick people.
3 A poe.......... is a short piece of writing. It may use special, beautiful language.
4 A novel.......... writes books with stories.
5 A build.......... makes things like houses, apartments and walls.
6 A sculpt.......... is a kind of art that people make—for example, with metal, wood or stone.
7 A dent.......... helps us to have healthy teeth.
8 A play.......... writes stories for the theater.

★ **(3)** **Complete the culture facts with the correct form of these words. There is one word you don't need.**

art	build	novel	photo	play	poem	~~sculpture~~

1 Antony Gormley is a British *sculptor*. His famous metal *Angel of the North* is 20 meters tall and 54 meters wide!
2 The .... Dante Alighieri was born in Florence, Italy. People have translated his poems into hundreds of languages.
3 Pablo Picasso was a famous Spanish .... He started painting when he was a child!
4 Shakespeare loved the theater. He was a .... and an actor. He also wrote poems.
5 The American .... Christopher Paolini started writing his first book, *Eragon*, when he was fifteen!
6 The Great Wall of China is the longest wall in the world. It took millions of .... to complete it!

Workbook page 119

★★ **(4)** **Complete the ads. Write a job or an art word in each blank.**

1
Do you want beautiful, white teeth?
At *WhiteSmile* you can find all the best *dentists* in town.

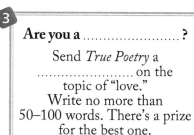

2
Today's World is looking for a new .... to take pictures for the newspaper. Can you take interesting, beautiful ....? Send us some examples.

3
Are you a ....?
Send *True Poetry* a .... on the topic of "love." Write no more than 50–100 words. There's a prize for the best one.

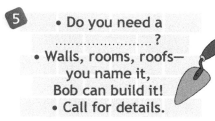

4
Come to the **SWAN THEATER** tonight to see Shakespeare's most famous .... about love, **ROMEO AND JULIET.**

5
• **Do you need a ....?**
• **Walls, rooms, roofs— you name it, Bob can build it!**
• **Call for details.**

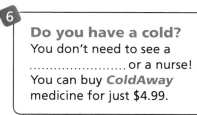

6
Do you have a cold?
You don't need to see a .... or a nurse! You can buy *ColdAway* medicine for just $4.99.

Speaking and Listening

★ **1** Read Harry's news. Mark (✓) the three correct responses.

> I just made it to the finals of *American Idol*!

Harry

Harry's friends:
1 I swear it's true!
2 No way!
3 You won't believe it!
4 Unbelievable!
5 I'm a lost cause!
6 You're kidding me!
7 Seriously.
8 What's up?

★ **2** Complete the conversation with these words. Then listen and check.
5

believe	kidding	Seriously
~~the best~~	true	Unbelievable
up	way	

Claire	Who was that on the phone? And why are you smiling?
Luke	Oh, it was my dad. I just heard ¹ *the best* news.
Claire	What's ² ....?
Luke	Well, you know that nature photography contest I entered?
Claire	I sure do! You sent in a photo of a blackbird, I remember.
Luke	Well, you won't ³ .... it, but I won!
Claire	No ⁴ .... !
Luke	⁵ .... I swear it's ⁶ .... And the first prize is a trip to the Grand Canyon!
Claire	⁷ .... ! You're so lucky. But it was a great photo. I'm a lost cause with a camera!
Luke	Hey, do you want to come? The prize is for four people, and Mom and Dad say I can bring a friend.
Claire	Really? You're ⁸ .... me. That would be amazing!

Speaking and Listening page 123

Brain Trainer

Listen to conversations in your Workbook and repeat them to improve your speaking skills.

Listen to recording 5 again and notice how the speakers emphasize words to show interest. Now read the conversation in Exercise 2 aloud, copying the intonation.

★★ **3** Listen to the conversation. Then correct
6 the mistakes in these sentences.

1 The conversation is between ~~two~~ *three* friends.
2 Zeke throws a basketball ....
   to Alice.
3 Zeke has written an article ....
4 He wrote it when he was in a café
   ....
5 Zeke's work is on page seventeen ....
6 It's about a missing child ....

★★ **4** Complete these extracts from the conversation.
6 Write one or two words in each blank. Listen
again and check.

A
Zeke I ¹ *just heard* some awesome news.
Tom So, come on, ² .... happened?
Alice Yeah, what's ³ .... ?
B
Zeke It's the "story of the week"!
Alice ⁴ .... way!
Tom You're ⁵ ....
Zeke Seriously. I ⁶ .... true.

★★ **5** Choose *one* of the situations in the pictures.
Imagine that this event just happened to you.
Write a conversation with a friend, giving your
news. Use expressions from Exercises 1, 2 and 4.

Grammar • Present perfect vs Past simple

★ **(1)** **We can complete sentences A and B in different ways. Match the sentence endings (1–6) to A or B.**

A I've lived here …
B We moved here …

1 _A._ all my life.
2 …. last summer.
3 …. in August.
4 …. for three years.
5 …. yesterday.
6 …. since 2000.

★ **(2)** **Choose the correct options in the news article.**

It's October 2011, and Fauja Singh [1] _just finished_ / _has just finished_ the Toronto Waterfront Marathon. He [2] _has started / started_ the marathon eight hours, twenty-five minutes and seventeen seconds ago!

Many people [3] _have already run / already ran_ much faster marathons. In April 2011, Geoffrey Mutai of Kenya [4] _has completed / completed_ the Boston marathon in two hours, three minutes and two seconds!

But on the day of the Toronto marathon, Fauja [5] _amazed / has amazed_ the world. Why? Well, no one [6] _has ever completed / completed_ a marathon at the age of 100 before!

Fauja [7] _has lived / lived_ in the US since 1992, but he [8] _was / has been_ born in India in 1911. He announced his retirement in 2013.

Grammar Reference pages 112–113

★★ **(3)** **Complete the Amazing Facts. Use the Present perfect or the Past simple form of these verbs.**

collect	complete	ever/wear	grow
~~love~~	put	take	travel

AMAZING FACTS
WORLD RECORDS

- Charlotte Lee has loved rubber ducks since she was a child. She [2] .... 5,631 rubber ducks in the last 18 years!
- [3] .... (you) two T-shirts at the same time? That's nothing! On November 13, 2011, Tom Rauen [4] .... on 247 T-shirts!
- In 2010, gardener Clare Pearce [5] .... a 119-centimeter-long cucumber in her greenhouse. She [6] .... a photo afterward, instead of eating it!
- Rob Thomson [7] .... abroad many times. In 2009 he [8] .... an around-the-world trip—by skateboard!

★★ **(4)** **a Make sentences with the Present perfect or the Past simple.**

1 I / never / meet / anyone famous
I've never met anyone famous.
2 A friend / already / tell / me that joke
A friend ....
3 I / make / an important decision / yesterday
I ....
4 My best friend / never / travel / abroad
My best friend ....
5 I / not do / anything exciting / last week
I ....
6 My parents / live / in this area / since they were born
My parents ....

b Which sentences in Exercise 4a are true for you?

Reading

1 Read the magazine article quickly. What's the oldest age people can send ideas?

50 Things to Do Before You're 18!

If you haven't turned eighteen yet, **MyWorld** magazine wants to hear from you! We want your suggestions for a **"50 things to do before you're 18"** list. Begin with the question **"Have you ever … ?"** We only want ideas you've already tried yourself!

Your replies

1 _c_ I've been amazed how quickly I've improved! It's really satisfying. I've been in my own band a year now, and we've even won a few contests! I've made tons of friends that way, too. Everyone you meet likes music, so you already have a lot to talk about. – **Catherine, Hot Springs**

2 …. Well, why not? Bad weather makes us sad, but this is a way to feel happy again. Yes, you do need to feel confident to try this! Some people have laughed at me, it's true—but many more have joined in! – **Ben, Seattle**

3 …. I can't believe there are people out there who've never seen the sun come up! You don't need to be a poet or an artist to find that beautiful. Oh, and this is an extra idea—go swimming with dolphins! I did it last summer and now I can't stop telling everyone how amazing it was. – **Lucy, Memphis**

4 …. Yesterday I helped to look for a man's dog. The day before that, I stood up when an older lady got on the bus, and I gave her my seat. These people weren't friends or family. They were simply people who needed help. And helping them made me feel great. Try it! It's pretty surprising. – **Prash, Minneapolis**

5 …. I've tried red, gothic black—and blue! I did it over summer break, so teachers didn't complain. (Warning: check that your parents are cool with this first! You don't want them to go crazy.) Or experiment with different clothes instead. It's great fun. There's plenty of time to look "serious" when you're an adult! – **Faith, Atlanta**

2 a Write questions. Begin with *Have you ever …* .

a dance / in the rain?

………………………………………………… ?

b change / the color of your hair?

………………………………………………… ?

c learn / how to play a musical instrument?

………………………………………………… ?

d stay / up all night?

………………………………………………… ?

e do / something nice for someone you don't know?

………………………………………………… ?

b Read the replies from *MyWorld* readers. Match the questions (a–e) to the emails (1–5).

3 What is similar about these suggestions?

They're all ways to
a be very successful
b feel good or happy
c impress your family or friends

4 Which idea do you like best?

Listening

1 Listen to the writer of one of the emails in Reading Exercise 1. Write the correct name.

7

2 Listen again. Mark (✓) the things the speaker has done.

7

1 visited Australia   4 been to a sports event
2 spoken to a celebrity   5 ridden a motorcycle
3 been on a scary ride   6 swum with sharks

3 Look at the ads. Which vacation activity do you think the speaker would be most interested in?

a **Go sightseeing in Rome on a photography tour**   ….

b **Learn a new language at our summer camp!**   ….

c **See the white tigers at the Atlanta Zoo**   ….

Writing • A biography

1 Read the biography quickly. How does Martha know her "hero"?

Martha is Ewa's ....

Inspirations and Heroes: we celebrate the people who've inspired you!

My Hero: Ewa Jarvis (my grandma) by **Martha Jarvis**

My grandma Ewa was born in Poland **in 1945**. She wanted to study cooking in college, but her family was poor, so **when** she was sixteen she started work in a factory. She hated it! She dreamed about baking.

Luckily, **a year later**, Ewa met my grandfather, Reggie, an American photographer. He loved her cooking! **The following year** they got married and moved to Chicago.

At that time, Ewa only spoke Polish. **During the day**, she worked in a café, and at night she studied. **After two years**, her English was excellent! **In 1971** my dad was born, and Ewa opened a bakery.

The bakery has been a big success. **A few years ago**, Ewa even made it to the finals of a TV cooking show! **Today** she's writing her own recipe book.

My grandma is my hero because she's made her dreams come true, and she's never given up. (Also, no one's ever made better apple pie ☺.)

2 Read the biography again. Put these events in order. Use the time expressions in bold in the biography to help you.

  a she did well in a cooking competition ....
  b she started writing a book ....
  c she met her future husband ....
  d she got a job in a café ....
  e she moved to the US ....
  f she got a job in a factory *1*
  g she started her own business ....
  h she spoke English really well for the first time ....

3 Complete the sentences. Use some of the words in bold from the biography in Exercise 1.

My hero, Matt Groening, was born in the US [1] *in* 1954. Like Bart Simpson, he didn't use to like school [2] .... he was young!

[3] .... 1972 he went to Evergreen State College. [4] .... his time at college, he decided to be a writer and artist. Five years [5] ...., he left Evergreen. [6] .... several months of doing some really terrible jobs (including cleaning tables!), he felt very tired, but he didn't give up. [7] .... following year he sold his first cartoon!

I watched my first Simpsons cartoon ten years [8] .... Since then, I've wanted to be a cartoonist, too!

4 You are going to write a biography of your hero for the *Inspirations and Heroes* website. Choose a person who's inspired you. Then take notes about his/her life.

Name ....
Born ....
Education/Family ....
....
Work ....
....
Other achievements ....
....
How/inspire/you ....
....

5 Write your biography. Use your notes from Exercise 4 and include at least four different time expressions.

....
....
....
....
....
....
....

3 Be Happy!

Vocabulary • Showing feelings

★ **1** Match the verbs (1–8) to the feelings (a–h).

1 cry	a hot
2 smile	b surprised
3 frown	c tired
4 blush	d upset
5 sweat	e cold
6 gasp	f embarrassed
7 yawn	g in a bad mood
8 shiver	h happy

★ **2** Choose the correct options.

1 I once *smiled / screamed* loudly during a scary movie.
2 I sometimes *shout / cry* when I read a sad book.
3 When my teacher gave me this homework, I *blushed / sighed*.
4 I never *frown / laugh* when someone falls down. It isn't funny!
5 I rarely *gasp / shout* when I'm angry. I'm usually pretty quiet.
6 Sometimes I *yawn / gasp* when I'm tired.

★ **3** Choose the correct options.

1 She cried when she failed her exams, because she was .... .
   a angry   b upset   c happy
2 Everyone laughed when I fell down. I felt .... , and I blushed!
   a fed up   b cold   c embarrassed
3 I was really .... when I won the lottery! I didn't believe it.
   a fed up   b frightened   c surprised
4 Tom was .... , so he went to bed early.
   a angry   b tired   c embarrassed
5 Ella is .... because we forgot her birthday. I feel terrible!
   a happy   b amused   c in a bad mood
6 It's rained all day! I'm bored and .... .
   a fed up   b hot   c amused

★★ **4** What's happening and why? Write sentences using the correct form of a verb from A and an adjective from B. There are two words in each list you don't need.

A	~~cry~~	frown	laugh	scream
	shiver	sigh	sweat	yawn

B	amused	bad	cold	embarrassed
	frightened	hot	tired	~~upset~~

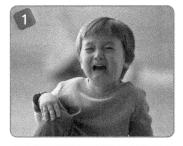

1 He's *crying because he's upset.*
2 She ....
3 He ....
4 They ....
5 She ....
6 He ....

Workbook page 120

Reading

1 Read the article quickly. Which description best describes the writer's general attitude toward "color psychology"?

a It sounds interesting.   b Don't believe it!

2 Read the article again. What does the writer say that the colors mean? Match 1–6 to a–f.

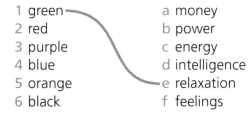

1 green   a money
2 red   b power
3 purple   c energy
4 blue   d intelligence
5 orange   e relaxation
6 black   f feelings

3 Read the text again and correct the sentences. Mark (✓) the sentence that is correct.

1 Green is a popular color in hospitals and ~~fast-food restaurants~~.
   Green is a popular color in hospitals and cafés.
2 It's a good idea to wear red for arguments.
   ....
3 The writer's bedroom used to be white.
   ....
4 "I'm feeling blue" means "I'm really happy."
   ....
5 The writer likes orange clothes.
   ....
6 Lawyers wear black because they want to look thin.
   ....

> **Brain Trainer**
>
> When you see a word or an expression you don't know, read the text carefully for clues about the meaning. Can you think of another word or expression that would fit the context?
>
> **Now do Exercise 4.**

4 Find these words and expressions in the article. Choose the best definition.

1 power (introduction) – ability / rule / emotion
2 be in trouble (red) – be happy / have problems / be in danger
3 symbolizes (purple) – looks / shows / means
4 be careful (blue) – think so you don't make a mistake / be free and happy / keep calm
5 booster (orange) – something that makes something worse / happier / better

Feeling Blue? by Carlos Martinez, psychologist

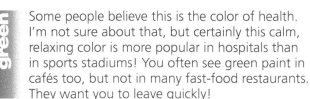

According to "color psychology," colors have the power to influence our feelings—and even our lives.

green Some people believe this is the color of health. I'm not sure about that, but certainly this calm, relaxing color is more popular in hospitals than in sports stadiums! You often see green paint in cafés too, but not in many fast-food restaurants. They want you to leave quickly!

red Red is a strong, energetic color. Wear it when you want to feel confident—for example, on a romantic date. Don't wear it if you're in trouble with a parent or teacher. Angry people are more likely to shout if they see red!

purple Hundreds of years ago, purple clothes were very expensive. Today the color still symbolizes wealth. Chinese Feng Shui experts believe that having purple in your home can make you rich, while red can bring good fortune. I just painted my boringly white bedroom both colors. Wish me luck!

blue Blue is popular with artists because it is the color of emotions. However, be careful. We don't say "I'm feeling blue" when we're laughing and smiling, but when we're fed up.

orange A friend told me that orange is a brain "booster"! I didn't believe her at first, but I tried it anyway. I look terrible in orange, so I put a lot of orange things on my desk instead. I think it helped! I felt happier, and I remembered more.

black Celebrities like black because it makes people look thinner! But it's also popular with people in authority, like lawyers and business people. That's because wearing black helps you to look strong and important. But *smile*. You don't want to look like Dracula!

Grammar • Gerunds and infinitives

★ 1 Complete the table with the examples.

> Dancing makes me happy. ~~I love swimming.~~
> I'm happy to cook. I'm tired of walking.
> I want to learn the guitar. I watch TV to relax.

Use a gerund (-*ing* form):
after certain verbs [1] *I love swimming.*
after prepositions [2] ....
as the subject or object of a sentence
[3] ....

Use an infinitive:
after certain verbs [4] ....
after certain adjectives [5] ....
to explain purpose [6] ....

★ 2 a Rania texts her friends the question "How are you?" Complete their replies.

1 Not so good. I hate *to do / doing* homework!
2 Good! It was great *to see / seeing* you last night.
3 I'm fed up with *to stay / staying* in. I'm so bored!
4 Tired! I want *to go / going* to bed, but it's only 9 p.m.!
5 Tired! But *to run / running* was great. I ran 7 km!
6 Bad day. I'm eating chocolate *to feel / feeling* better!

b Read the texts again and answer the question.

How many people are feeling positive? ☺
....

★★ 3 Complete the text. Use the correct gerund or infinitive form of the verbs.

How to make friends and influence people!
1 Try *to sound* (sound) positive. Most of us prefer .... (spend) time with happy people!
2 Start a conversation by .... (ask) questions.
3 It's very important .... (listen), too.
4 .... (lie) is a bad idea. Be honest!
5 Look into someone's eyes .... (show) interest.
6 Remember .... (smile)!

★★ 4 Complete the sentences (1–6). Then match them to the situations (A–F).

> ~~cry~~   feel   go   lie   play   shout

1 Cheer up. *Crying* doesn't help.   C
2 I hate .... Please calm down!   ....
3 It's too cold! I don't want .... this game anymore.   ....
4 I'm scared of .... to the dentist. It hurts!   ....
5 This is relaxing! I'd be happy .... here all morning.   ....
6 When I'm sad I sometimes eat junk food .... better.   ....

Grammar Reference pages 114–115

Vocabulary • Adjective suffixes

★ (1) a **Complete the table with the adjectives.**

noun + suffix (-ful, -ous or -y) → adjective	
health	¹ *healthy*
luck	² ....
wealth	³ ....
danger	⁴ ....
fame	⁵ ....
poison	⁶ ....
peace	⁷ ....
success	⁸ ....
beauty	⁹ ....

b **Which two adjectives have a mainly negative meaning?**

.... and ....

★ (2) **Choose the correct options.**

1 I'm not interested in being *fame* /*famous*.
2 Stop! Don't drink that *poison / poisonous*!
3 It's important to take care of your *health / healthy*.
4 I dream of being *wealth / wealthy* one day.
5 You need a lot of *luck / lucky* to be famous.
6 I live in a small, *peace / peaceful* town.

★ (3) a **Complete the life advice with the adjective form of the nouns. Use the suffixes -ful, -ous and -y.**

1 ❝ It's better to be happy than to be *wealthy* (wealth). ❞

2 ❝ .... (success) people believe in themselves. ❞

3 ❝ Being .... (beauty) is less important than being nice. ❞

4 ❝ If you're happy and .... (health), you're rich. ❞

5 ❝ Having too much money can be .... (danger). ❞

6 ❝ If you want to be .... (fame), you need to work hard, have a lot of talent— and be very, very .... (luck). ❞

b **Which piece of advice do you like best?**

Workbook page 120

★★ (4) **Complete the star sign personality profiles with the adjective form of the nouns.**

beauty	danger	~~fame~~	health
luck	peace	success	wealth

Aries , Leo , Sagittarius

People with these star signs love attention! They dream of being ¹ *famous*, like celebrities. They like exciting, ² .... hobbies, like surfing and climbing. They rarely get scared!

Gemini , Libra , Aquarius

People with these star signs are often ³ .... people—bad luck rarely comes their way! They are usually very ⁴ .... because they enjoy exercise and good food.

Cancer , Scorpio , Pisces

People with these star signs are often ⁵ ...., quiet people. They don't like shouting! They like looking at ⁶ .... things, like paintings, or enjoying music and poetry.

Taurus , Virgo , Capricorn

People with these star signs are often ⁷ .... at school and work because they try hard to make their dreams come true. They're often ⁸ .... because they're good with money.

★★ (5) a **Complete the people's dreams with the correct noun or adjective form of these words.**

~~fame~~	peace	poison	success	wealth

1 Zak: I dream about *fame*. I want to be a celebrity!
2 Ana: I want to help protect the environment from .... chemicals.
3 Tim: I want to end war and fighting, and help create .... on earth.
4 Tillie: I hope I become .... so that I can buy a lot of nice things!
5 Hasan: I want to be .... , like my parents. My dad's a doctor, and my mom's a famous playwright.

b **Write your own dream.**

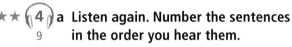

Chatroom Invitations

Speaking and Listening

★ (1) **Complete the table with these words and expressions.**

| ~~feel like~~ like I'd I have to I'll I'm want |

Inviting
Do you ¹ *feel like* + -ing?
Do you ² .... to … ?
Would you ³ .... to … ?
Accepting
That's a great idea. ⁴ .... love to!
Sure! Thanks. ⁵ .... see you there.
Declining
That sounds like fun, but ⁶ ....
sorry, I can't.
Sorry. ⁷ .... say no.

★ (2) **Complete the phone conversation with the**
8 **correct options. Then listen and check.**

Ali Hi, Rosa, it's Ali. Do you ¹(feel like)/ want going bowling tonight?

Rosa Hi, Ali! That sounds like fun, but I'm sorry, ² *I can't / I'd love to.* I have to do homework tonight.

Ali Really? Oh, OK.

Rosa ³ *Would you like to / Do you feel like* see the new Pixar movie?

Ali That's a great idea. ⁴ *I'd love to! / I'm sorry.* Do you ⁵ *want / feel like* going on Saturday?

Rosa Sorry. ⁶ *I have to / I'd love to* say no. It's my dad's birthday that night. Do you ⁷ *like / want* to go tonight at 7:30?

Ali Sure! Thanks. ⁸ *I'll / I'd* see you there. Hey, wait! Aren't you doing homework tonight?

Rosa Oh, yeah. But only for a little while. Sorry, Ali. The truth is, I really hate bowling!

★★ (3) **Listen to a phone conversation.**
9 **Then answer the questions.**

1 What does Bella want to play with Nick?
basketball

2 What has Nick hurt? ....

3 How old is Nick's sister? ....

4 What are Bella and Nick going to eat tonight?
....

5 What *doesn't* Bella like? ....

★★ (4) a **Listen again. Number the sentences**
9 **in the order you hear them.**

a That's a great idea. I'd love to! ....
....

b Sure! Thanks. I'll see you then. ....
....

c How about watching a movie? ....
....

d Do you want to play basketball this
afternoon? *1.* ......*inviting*......

e Sorry, but I have to say no. ....
....

f That sounds like fun, but I'm sorry, I can't. ....
....

g Would you like to hang out later? ....
....

b **For each sentence, write *inviting*, *accepting*, or *declining*.**

★★ (5) **Write a conversation with a friend. Use the ideas below and phrases from Exercises 1–4.**

• invite your friend to do something fun this weekend. (What? When?)
  ↓
  • your friend can't go. (Why not?)
    ↓
  • invite your friend to do another activity at a different time.
    ↓
    • your friend can go!
Possible activities (or use your own ideas!)

| ride bikes | go shopping |
| go for a walk |
| play video games | go swimming |

Speaking and Listening page 124

Grammar • Present perfect continuous

★ 1 Match 1–6 to a–f to make short conversations.

1 You look tired.   *e*
2 Why are you shivering?
3 Why are you laughing?
4 Why are you so angry with me?
5 You're sweating!
6 You look surprised.

a Oh, Luna's been telling us jokes for the last half hour!
b Why? I've been waiting for you all day!
c I've been standing in the cold for an hour!
d Yes. Your teacher has been telling us what a good student you are!
e I am. We've been working all evening.
f Are we? Sorry! Jo's been playing tennis with me.

★ 2 Complete the sentences with the Present perfect continuous form of the verbs.

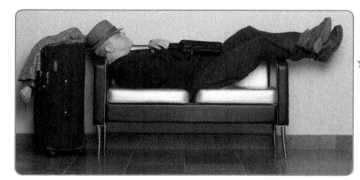

1 *Have you been waiting* (you/wait) long?
2 I'm fed up. It .... (rain) all day.
3 She's really happy with her test scores. She .... (smile) all afternoon!
4 I can't sleep! My neighbors .... (play) loud music all evening.
5 I'm really tired. I .... (not sleep) well these past few days.
6 Mr. Green is in a bad mood this morning. He .... (frown) for hours.
7 I don't think she's enjoying my poem. She .... (yawn) since I started reading it!
8 Why are you shivering? What .... (you/do)?

★★ 3 Phoebe's been having a party! But there's a problem. Read what she says, then complete the guests' replies. Use the Present perfect continuous form of these verbs.

| blush   clean   dance   ~~play~~   sit   talk   watch |

Phoebe I'm really angry. Someone just broke my mom's favorite vase. Who did it?
Beth It wasn't me! ¹ *I've been playing* computer games all night.
Mark It wasn't me! I ² .... in this chair for hours.
Layla Maybe it was Dan? He ³ .... to music all night!
Tom It wasn't Josie. She ⁴ .... up in the kitchen all evening.
Olivia Don't look at me! I ⁵ .... to Tom for the last half hour. We haven't moved!
Arthur Maybe it was your brother? I ⁶ .... him since you asked your question. He ⁷ .... the whole time!

★★ 4 What's been happening? Read the conversations. Complete the replies. Use the Present perfect continuous form of appropriate verbs.

1 **A** You all look fed up!
  B We are! We*'ve been doing* homework for hours!
2 **A** Why does your dad have paint all over his clothes?
  B He .... my bedroom. Do you want to take a look?
3 **A** Why are my books all over the floor?
  B Sorry. We .... them.
4 **A** You look very hot!
  B I am! I .... aerobics. I don't think I'm in good shape!
5 **A** What's that noise?
  B It's my sister. She .... awful rock music all afternoon.
6 **A** Why is the kitchen such a mess?
  B Sorry! I .... a cake for Ella's birthday. I'll clean up now!

Grammar Reference pages 114–115

Reading

1 Read the web article quickly. Match the jobs to the photos. There is one photo you don't need.

Unusual Jobs

← → C 🏠

| HOME | NEWS | FEATURES | PHOTOS | COMMENTS |

Unusual Jobs Part 9: Jobs That Make People Laugh! ▶▶

A ▶▶ I've been working as a professional clown for almost two years. Before that, I was a comedian for nine years. I was never famous, but I was pretty successful! I changed jobs because I wanted to do more in life than make people laugh. What if I could help people, too?

As a clown, I try to encourage sick children in the hospital to laugh and smile. When you laugh, your mind and body relax. Apparently, people who laugh more don't suffer from as many colds or other problems! Children who laugh a lot often do better in school, too.

It isn't an easy job. Not all sick children get better, and sometimes I come home and cry. But I always go back to work the next day with my red nose on. I don't earn a lot of money as a clown, but I feel very lucky to work with such brave, wonderful patients.

B ▶▶ I became a laughter yoga teacher more than three years ago. I was originally a dentist! My old job was very difficult, and I used to feel fed up. Now I still improve people's health, but everything else is completely different. Everyone has fun in a laughter yoga class, including the teacher!

No, laughter isn't "magic." It doesn't prevent all illnesses, keep you young or make you beautiful. But did you know that it's an excellent kind of exercise? You move your whole body when you laugh!

Sometimes I work with celebrities. It's true that being rich can be stressful! Famous people can be unpleasant at times, but I try to change their bad moods. Laughter is excellent for people like musicians, artists and writers because it helps them to be more creative.

2 Read the article again. Answer the questions. Write *A*, *B*, *both* or *neither*.

1 Who has done his/her job for three years?   *B*
2 Who has been making people laugh for more than ten years?
3 Who has been famous?
4 Who has a job related to health?
5 Who sometimes feels sad at work?
6 Who doesn't always like the people he/she works with?

3 According to the texts in Exercise 1, what are the benefits of laughter? Mark (✓) five ideas.

1 more happiness
2 better study skills
3 more beautiful appearance
4 less stress
5 more fitness
6 no illnesses
7 more artistic ability
8 more wealth

Listening

1 Listen to a radio show. 10 Complete the tip sheet heading.

> ### Tips for times when you ....!
>
> **1** The best time to go to bed is *ten o'clock*.
> **2** Most people need to sleep for around .... to .... hours a night.
> **3** When you're tired, drink ....
> **4** Exercise in the .... or in the ....
> **5** Eating dark .... can help.
> **6** Do something fun, like ....

2 Listen again. Complete the tips. 10 Can you add any more ideas?

Writing • A "for and against" essay

1 Read the title of the essay in Exercise 2. Then read the student's notes. Are these arguments for or against the topic?

> 1 more people to talk to? *for*
> 2 smaller number of very good friends—more important? ....
> 3 making friends online can be dangerous? ....
> 4 don't need to feel bored—always someone to talk to? ....
> 5 not healthy to spend more time socializing on Internet than in real life? ....

2 Read the essay. Which idea in Exercise 1 is not used?

> **Having a lot of friends on social networking sites is important for happiness.**
>
> Some people have a lot of friends online, but does that mean they are happy?
>
> Having friends helps us to feel good. Friends laugh with us, and they share dreams and ideas. They listen to us when we feel upset, too. People with a lot of friends on social networking sites always have someone to talk to online, so they don't feel bored. Additionally, when we have a lot of friends, we feel important and special.
>
> On the other hand, some people spend more time chatting with friends on the Internet than they do in real life. Our online friends aren't always "real" friends. Some people don't see their online friends very often.
>
> In conclusion, having friends on social networking sites can help us to feel happy. However, we also need to have friends in real life. What's more, having one or two really good friends can be better than having a lot of friends we don't know very well!

3 Read the essay again. Complete the table with the correct linking words.

Addition
¹ *and*   ² a......................   ³ t......................
⁴ A......................

Contrast
⁵ b......................   ⁶ H......................
⁷ O......................

Brain Trainer

Always take short notes before you write. Write down as many ideas as you can. Then choose the best ones.
Now do Exercise 4.

4 a Read the essay title below. Are notes 1–6 for or against the topic?

> **Living out in the country is important for happiness**
>
> **1** living somewhere beautiful—feel happy *for*
> **2** more peaceful—less stressed ....
> **3** less exciting—more boring ....
> **4** meeting people and making friends—more difficult ....
> **5** "green" places—good for health ....
> **6** movies, malls, etc.—travel a long way ....

b Do you agree?

5 You are going to write an essay with the same title. Write your ideas below.

Paragraph 1: Introduction ....
....

Paragraph 2: Arguments for ....
....

Paragraph 3: Arguments against ....
....

Paragraph 4: Conclusion and your opinion ....
....

6 Now write your "for and against" essay using the title in Exercise 4. Use the ideas and paragraph plan in Exercises 1–5. Include linking words of addition and contrast.

....
....
....
....
....
....
....
....
....

Check 1

Grammar

1. Complete the email with the correct form of the verbs.

New Message   ⊗

Hi there Kayla,   [Send]
How's it going? I ⁰ *'ve been having* (have)
an interesting day so far!
Earlier today, I ¹........................ (go) to the mall
to do some shopping. While I ²........................
(walk) down Ash Street, I noticed a wallet on
the ground. Luckily, there was a cell phone
number inside.
The owner, Chris, sounded really happy when
I called. "I ³........................ (look) for my wallet
for hours and hours!" he said. We decided
⁴........................ (meet) at a coffee shop.
When I first saw Chris, he ⁵........................ (sit)
with his back to me, so I didn't recognize him
at first. But when I got closer, I saw it was Chris
Harper—you know, that awful boy we
⁶........................ (used to/hate) in elementary
school! He ⁷........................ (change) a lot
since then. He ⁸........................ (not used to/be)
very friendly, but today I really enjoyed
⁹........................ (talk) to him. In fact,
I ¹⁰........................ (think) about him nonstop
since then. I hope he liked me, too!
Anyway, call me soon. I think I need some
advice about what to do next!
Eloise xx

/ 10 points

2. Rewrite the second sentence so that it has a similar meaning to the first one. Use between three and five words, including the word in parentheses.

0 The last time I went surfing was two
  years ago.   (been)
  I *haven't been surfing for* two years.
1 I didn't like school when I was young.   (use)
  I .... school when
  I was young.
2 He moved to Dallas two years ago.   (living)
  He ....
  for two years.
3 This is my first time on a steamboat!   (never)
  I ....
  on a steamboat before.
4 Having such amazing friends makes me feel
  lucky.   (have)
  I feel ....
  such amazing friends.
5 The last time I saw Sarah was Friday.   (haven't)
  I .... Friday.

/ 5 points

Vocabulary

3. Choose the correct options.

I can't wait until you ⁰ *go / get / give*
back. Please ¹ *make / go / keep* in touch!

I'm bored and fed ² *on / with / up*. Can I go
and ³ *hang / keep / get* out with my friends?

Can you help? I'm looking ⁴ *at / for / to* my
dog. He ⁵ *gone / kept / ran* away!

/ 5 points

4 Complete the definitions with appropriate words.

0 A c*lassmate* is another student in your class.
1 When you feel embarrassed, you b......................... (your face goes red).
2 A l......................... has a strong light that guides ships.
3 Some people frown when they're in a bad m......................... .
4 If you k......................... calm, you don't panic or go crazy.
5 Each town has at least one f......................... . He/She puts fires out.

/ 5 points

5 Write the correct adjective or noun form of the word.

Historic figures

Leonardo da Vinci

Leonardo da Vinci was a very talented man! He was not only an ⁰*artist* (art), but also a ¹.........................(sculpture), musician, scientist, mathematician, writer, ².........................(poem)—and a ³.........................(wealth) business person! Da Vinci's ⁴...................(beauty) painting, the *Mona Lisa*, is probably the most ⁵.........................(fame) portrait in the world.

/ 5 points

Speaking

6 Complete the conversation with these words.

| do | happened | ~~most~~ | so (x2) | Sorry |
| such | to | true | way | would |

Cal   Hey, Leah, I just heard the ⁰*most* incredible news!
Leah Really? What ¹......................... ?
Cal   We've made it to the finals of the school band competition!
Leah No ²......................... ! You're kidding me.
Cal   Seriously, I swear it's ³......................... . I was ⁴......................... surprised when Tara told me, I think I gasped! She must think I'm ⁵......................... an idiot.
Leah Probably …
Cal   Thanks! So, anyway, ⁶......................... you want to come over tonight to practice?
Leah ⁷......................... . I have to say no. I have ⁸......................... much homework to do!
Cal   Well, ⁹.........................you like to come over on Saturday instead?
Leah I'd love ¹⁰......................... ! I'll see you then!

/ 10 points

Translation

7 Translate the sentences.

1 We used to live in a farmhouse near a windmill.
....
2 Have you ever been on a speedboat or a motorcycle?
....
3 The babysitter screamed while she was watching a horror movie.
....
4 I want to find out how to help people and make a difference.
....
5 She's yawning because she's been setting up for the party all day.
....

/ 5 points

Dictation

8 Listen and write.

11
1 ....
2 ....
3 ....
4 ....
5 ....

/ 5 points

Survive!

Vocabulary • Natural disasters

 1 Find natural disaster words in the word search.
Then match the words to the definitions (1–8).

V	O	L	C	A	N	O	X	S	O	K
S	E	A	R	T	H	Q	U	A	K	E
R	B	O	G	U	H	T	J	R	A	H
I	A	V	A	L	A	N	C	H	E	G
Z	D	S	X	I	K	I	Q	G	H	J
C	H	P	N	D	I	S	E	A	S	E
Z	H	U	R	R	I	C	A	N	E	X
U	R	M	T	S	U	N	A	M	I	O
R	W	L	G	J	F	L	O	O	D	L
F	A	N	A	O	F	A	M	I	N	E

1 What happens when people die from hunger:
f *amine*
2 A storm with very strong winds:
h........................
3 A disaster that moves the earth:
e........................
4 A very big, dangerous wave: t........................
5 A mountain that erupts: v........................
6 What happens when rivers and oceans get
too full: f........................
7 A bad illness that spreads from one person
to another: d........................
8 What happens when snow or rocks fall down
a mountain: a........................

Brain Trainer

When you learn new verbs, find out if they are regular
or irregular. It is a good idea to record any irregular past
forms, like this: fall (verb), fell (Past simple), fallen
(past participle).

Now do Exercise 2. Which verb has an irregular
past tense?

Workbook page 121

★ **2** Choose the correct options.

1 Some animals and plants can't (survive) / *spread*
in very hot weather.
2 In 1928 Mount Etna *drowned* / *erupted* with
smoke and hot, melted rocks.
3 Hot rocks and lava fell on Mascali and *buried* /
starved the town in 1928.
4 In 1846–50, a million Irish people *starved* /
drowned because they didn't have enough food.
5 When the Doña Paz hit another ship in 1987,
4,375 people *destroyed* / *drowned*.
6 The Great Fire of London *erupted* / *destroyed*
13,200 houses in 1666.

★★ **3** Match the captions (1–6) to the pictures (a–f).
Then write the name of the natural disaster.

avalanche	drought	~~earthquake~~
famine	flood	volcano

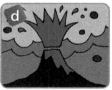  

1 It destroyed parts of the city. _f._
Disaster: ....*earthquake*....
2 Look! It's burying the town! ....
Disaster: ....
3 Help them! They're starving! ....
Disaster: ....
4 It's erupting! ....
Disaster: ....
5 Save it before it drowns! ....
Disaster: ....
6 It didn't survive. ....
Disaster: ....

Reading

★ **1** **Read the article quickly. Choose the correct option to complete the first sentence.**

   a … teaches people how to sail boats.

   b … saves lives at sea.

   c … researches extreme ocean weather.

★ **2** **Read the article again and complete the fact file.**

> **The RNLI: key facts**
> **1** "RNLI" means *Royal National Lifeboat Institution*.
> **2** The charity helps people around Britain and
> ....
> **3** Around .... volunteers work for the RNLI.
> **4** The charity has existed since ....
> **5** RNLI owns around .... lifeboats.
> **6** It rescues around .... people every day.

★ **3** **Choose the correct options.**

1 What do we learn about the RNLI?
   a It's one of the four official emergency services in the UK.
   b It's one of the biggest emergency services.
   c It doesn't pay any of the people who work for it.

2 What do we learn about Joy?
   a She sometimes surprises people.
   b She joined the RNLI more than four years ago.
   c She is one of the first female volunteers.

3 What do we learn about the UK?
   a It never has hurricanes.
   b It sometimes has earthquakes.
   c It will never have a tsunami.

4 What do we learn about tombstoning?
   a It is popular everywhere in the UK.
   b People try to jump onto rocks.
   c Some people have died after trying it.

★ **4** **Do you think Joy would agree with these statements? Write ✓ or ✗.**

1 I don't have any heroes.   ✗
2 I hope more women volunteer.
3 I sometimes feel frightened.
4 I think the RNLI costs far too much.
5 I'm always happy at work.
6 I always try to rescue everyone.

The Fourth Emergency Service?

The Royal National Lifeboat Institution (RNLI) is a charity that ..... . It operates around Britain and Ireland. After the police, fire and ambulance services, it's the largest emergency service in the UK, although not an official one. Many of the people who work for the RNLI are volunteers.

Joy Thomas is one of around 40,000 volunteers. "I've worked for the RNLI for almost four years," she says. "I've rescued over fifty people. At first, they're happy to see me. But afterward, they often express surprise. I think they expect to see an old man with a beard! However, 8% of RNLI lifeboat volunteers are women. As long ago as 1838, the amazing Grace Dent saved 13 people from drowning. More should follow her example!"

Since the RNLI began in 1824, it has saved more than 139,000 lives. That figure often shocks people, because the UK isn't famous for extreme weather. "We don't often have hurricanes, and we only experience tiny earthquakes, so tsunamis are unlikely," says Joy, "but that doesn't mean our coasts are safe, especially in storms and floods. Rescuers must be extremely careful, as sailing in these conditions is really scary."

The RNLI has to spend $659,000 every day on its 444 lifeboats and other services. "But we save around 22 lives a day, which is worth any price," says Joy. "And the people we rescue don't have to pay anything."

"I'll help anyone in trouble," she adds, "but stupid behavior does make me angry sometimes! There are parts of the country where young people go 'tombstoning'—they jump from high cliffs into the ocean. They can't see the deep waters or the rocks below. You really shouldn't try this dangerous hobby! Sadly, not everyone survives."

Grammar • Modals: ability, obligation, prohibition, advice

★ **1** **Read the sentences (1–6). Match the verbs in bold to the meanings (a–f).**

1 Luckily, I **can** climb really well.   *b*
2 You **should** keep calm. You **shouldn't** panic.
3 I **can't** swim. Help!
4 We **must** leave now. We **have to** hurry!
5 You **don't have to** take the class if you don't want to.
6 You **mustn't** hunt the animals. It isn't allowed!

a obligation
b ability
c prohibition
d no ability
e advice
f no obligation

Brain Trainer

Have to, must, don't have to and *mustn't* often cause problems for English learners. Write example sentences to help you to remember the differences.

have to and *must* = obligation
You **have to/must** wear a seatbelt. It's the law.

BUT *don't have to* = no obligation
You **don't have to (mustn't)** carry a first-aid kit. It's optional.

mustn't = prohibition
You **mustn't (don't have to)** drive without a license. It's illegal.

Now do Exercise 2.

★ **2** **Choose the correct options.**

1 You .... go home. It's getting late.
   (a) should   b can   c mustn't
2 Help him! He .... swim!
   a shouldn't   b can't   c don't have to
3 You .... stay on the main path, but it's a good idea.
   a shouldn't   b mustn't   c don't have to
4 You .... go out without your cell phone. What if you get lost?
   a don't have to   b can't   c shouldn't
5 I've broken my leg. You .... leave me here alone!
   a mustn't   b can   c don't have to

• Past modals

★ **3** **Complete the text with the Past simple of the verbs.**

By the end of my first skiing vacation, I ¹ *could* (can) ski, but I ² .... (can't) ski very fast! I ³ .... (have to) be careful, but I ⁴ .... (not have to) stay in the beginners area.

★★ **4** **Complete the campsite notices. Choose the most appropriate modal verb.**

~~can~~	can	can't
could	didn't have to	don't have to
must	mustn't	should

1 If you *can* ride a bike, why not join one of our biking trips? (No excuses—if you .... ride a bike when you were five, you still .... now!)

2 If you enjoy delicious food, you .... visit our diner. We strongly recommend it!

3 You .... play music after 11 p.m. It's against camp rules.

4 You .... pay for maps. They're free!

5 Please don't use the pool if you .... swim.

6 You .... keep the campsite neat and clean, or we will ask you to pay a $20 fine. Last year our campers were all very responsible, and we .... fine anyone. Thank you for your cooperation! ☺

Grammar Reference pages 116–117

Vocabulary • Phrasal verbs 2

1 a Choose the correct prepositions.

1 I've run out *of* / *over* / *through* food. ☹
2 I got *down* / *on* / *through* all my exams with no problems.
3 I'm looking forward *to* / *off* / *on* tomorrow.
4 I've fallen *across* / *down* / *on*.
5 My motorcycle has broken *down* / *over* / *out*.
6 I've figured *across* / *down* / *out* the answer.
7 I can't keep *on* / *through* / *over* going!
8 I was stressed at first, but now I've calmed *over* / *down* / *off*.

b Who is having problems? Write (☹).

2 Complete the calls for help with the correct form of these verbs.

break	come	figure	~~get~~	run

1 **A** I'm so tired. I don't think I can *get* through this.
   B Yes, you can! Don't fall asleep. Help is coming.
2 **A** I'm lost! I can't .... out where I am.
   B Look around you. Tell me what you can see.
3 **A** We just .... across a huge poisonous snake.
   B You mustn't go near it! Walk away slowly.
4 **A** My car has .... down on the highway!
   B You should get out and wait in a safe place nearby.
5 **A** I've .... out of water.
   B Can you see a river or a pond anywhere?

3 Complete the text. Write one preposition in each blank.

We hope you're looking forward ¹ *to* your camping vacation.

Don't forget to pack these essentials:

✱ a map and compass so you can always figure ² .... where you are.
✱ a first-aid kit. It's useful if someone falls ³ .... or gets sick.
✱ a lot of food so you don't run ⁴ .... Remember, the nearest store might be kilometers away!
✱ sunscreen and a hat to put ⁵ .... if it's hot.
✱ a good camera or camera phone to take photos when you come ⁶ .... something interesting.

★★ 4 Answer the questions about the pictures. Use the correct form of a verb from list A and a preposition from list B to make phrasal verbs.

A	break	~~come~~	fall	put	run	take

B	~~across~~	down (x2)	off	on	out of

What just happened?

1 I *just came across a snake.*

2 She ....
....

3 Our ....
....

4 He ....
....

What's happening at the moment?

5 She ....
....

6 I ....
....

Workbook page 121

Speaking and Listening

★ 1 What do we say *after* we've completely understood something?

a Are you saying that … ?
b Oh, I see!
c What do you mean?

★ 2 Complete the conversation with the correct form of these verbs. Then listen and check.

12

> Hurry   mean   say   see   ~~swim~~   understand

Jess Hey, get out of the water! You shouldn't ¹*swim* in the ocean.

Rory Sorry, I don't ²........................ . Are you ³........................ that the ocean is dangerous?

Jess Yes! There are jellyfish!

Rory What do you ⁴........................ ? Jellyfish aren't dangerous.

Jess Some kinds of jellyfish are! They can sting you. It really hurts!

Rory Oh, I ⁵........................ ! Thanks. OK, I'm coming.

Jess Good. ⁶........................ up!

★ 3 Match the phrases (a–f) to the blanks (1–6) in the conversation. What is the problem?

Ben Stop!

Daisy ¹*b* ! That hurt!

Ben Sorry! ².... . I wanted to stop you before you took a bite!

Daisy Sorry, ³.... . What's the problem? ⁴.... ? I thought it was for everyone.

Ben No, it isn't mine. But I should warn you— Mom made it!

Daisy ⁵.... ? Does your mom want to eat it all?

Ben No, but she's a terrible cook! You might not survive!

Daisy ⁶.... ! Thanks for the warning! I think I'll have some chips, then.

a Are you saying that it's *your* cake
b Ouch
c Oh, I see
d I don't understand
e What do you mean
f But you shouldn't eat that cake

★★ 4 Listen to a conversation. Which image best matches Freya's map?

13

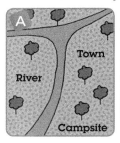
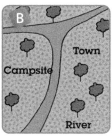
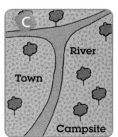

★★ 5 Listen to the conversation again. Why does Jack make these statements? Match the statements (1–5) to the explanations (a–g). There are two explanations you don't need.

13

1 Ouch!   *d*
2 Hurry up!
3 Are you saying that you want to go back to the campsite?
4 It isn't right? What do you mean?
5 Oh, I see! Thanks.

a He doesn't understand why the sign is wrong.
b He is feeling hungry.
c He understands what Freya means.
d He has hurt his foot.
e He doesn't understand why Freya wants him to stop walking.
f He disagrees that they need to call for help.
g He is feeling cold.

★★ 6 Write a conversation between two friends using the ideas below.

• you / not drink from the river – dangerous

  • sorry / not understand – you / say / dangerous animals / here?

    • no / but water / not safe

      • what / mean?

• dirty – sometimes people get diseases from / drink / dirty water

  • oh / see! Thanks.

Speaking and Listening page 125

Grammar • Modals: possibility

★ 1 Look at the photo. Then read the sentences (1–8). Does the writer think these things are possible (?), impossible (✗) or certain (✓)?

1 It might be a pet. *?*
2 He can't be scared of spiders.
3 He could like other kinds of insects.
4 He must be brave!
5 It might run up his arm!
6 It must feel strange.
7 It can't be a poisonous spider.
8 It could bite him!

★ 2 a Choose the correct options to complete the advertisement.

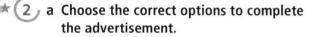

Storm Chaser Tours

Vacations tend to be similar—and boring! You ¹ *might / must* go to the beach, or you ² *could / can't* visit a few museums. Yawn! Doing the same thing every year ³ *must / can't* be very exciting!

Chasing tornadoes ⁴ *can't / must* be one of the most exciting vacation experiences in the world. We're 100% sure! You'll see these amazing storms close up, and if you're lucky, you ⁵ *must / might* have some great photos to take home.

Additionally, our tours are the cheapest in the US. We ⁶ *can't / must* be crazy!

b Would you like this vacation? Why?/Why not?

Grammar Reference pages 116–117

★★ 3 Complete the sentences about the photo with *might*, *must* or *can't*. Then answer the question below.

1 She *might* be in the Alps. I'm not sure.
2 She definitely .... be afraid of heights!
3 She .... enjoy climbing, or she wouldn't do it!
4 It looks very dangerous. There .... be an avalanche!
5 She .... be cold in all that snow!
6 Climbing that mountain .... be easy. It looks impossible!
7 She .... feel frightened. We don't know.
8 Standing on the top of a mountain .... be an amazing feeling, that's for sure.

Which sentences can you rewrite with *could*?

★★ 4 Rewrite the sentences using *must*, *can't*, *might* or *could*. Sometimes there may be more than one correct answer.

1 It's possible it's a tsunami.
   It *could be a tsunami.*
2 I'm sure the disease is very painful.
   The disease ....
3 Perhaps the volcano is dangerous.
   The volcano ....
4 I'm not going to climb that mountain. Obviously, you think I'm an idiot!
   I'm not going to climb that mountain.
   You .... !
5 It's impossible for a drought to last forever.
   A drought ....
6 Maybe she's lost in the forest.
   She ....
7 I don't believe that anyone enjoys this awful weather—not even you!
   You .... ! I don't believe you!

Reading

1 **Read the profile quickly. Find five animals.**

1 f *ox*
2 r.......................
3 a.......................
4 w.......................
5 f.......................h
6 s.......................

PROFILE

Ray Mears
Survival Expert

Ray Mears is an English TV star and survival expert. ª .5. A young Ray wanted to explore local forests because he was interested in animals, especially foxes. However, he couldn't afford camping equipment. ᵇ....

In 1994 he appeared on his first TV show. ᶜ.... These have been very popular because they're really exciting. Ray doesn't just tell us how to survive. He shows us! On a typical show, we might see him digging for water in a drought, for example, or hunting a rabbit for dinner.

Unlike other TV hosts, Ray is more interested in teaching us than shocking us. So he doesn't do crazy things, like wrestling alligators! He believes that people who want to survive mustn't do anything dangerous. But we probably wouldn't want to try all of his ideas. Some of them aren't very attractive! For instance, Ray believes that worms can be excellent food if you're hungry. ᵈ....

Ray Mears believes that everyone should learn some basic survival skills. ᵉ.... For example, imagine you get lost on a walk. What would you do? On his UK survival courses, Ray teaches children and adults how to make a fire, find water and even catch fish, among many other things!

In 2009 three young British tourists named Chiara, Rachel and Rory got lost in a forest in Malaysia. They were hungry, wet and scared of the dangerous snakes. Luckily, Rory liked watching TV! ᶠ.... The friends followed a river until it reached the coast, where they found help. They survived—thanks to Ray!

Brain Trainer

Writers often use pronouns and possessive adjectives (e.g., *I, she, ours, his, that, those, some*) to refer back to people, places, times and things they have already mentioned. Read the previous sentences in the text to find out what these pronouns and possessive adjectives are referring to.
Now do Exercise 2.

2 **Read the sentences. What do the words in bold refer to? Use ideas from the box. Then match the sentences to the blanks (a–f) in the profile.**

1994	a worm	camping equipment
~~Ray Mears's~~	Rory	survival skills

1 Instead, Ray worked out how to spend nights outside without **it** (.......................)!
2 **He** (.......................) remembered some advice from a Ray Mears's TV show.
3 But I don't think I'm going to try **one** (.......................) very soon!
4 One day, **they** (.......................) could save our lives!
5 **His** (*Ray Mears's*) interest in survival began in childhood.
6 Since **then** (.......................), Ray's starred in over ten different shows.

Listening

1
14 **Listen to four short recordings. Match the contexts (a–d) to the recordings (1–4).**

a conversation between friends   *2*
b travel announcement
c instructions from a tour guide
d news show

2
14 **Listen again. Complete the problems with natural disaster words. Then complete the advice and warnings.**

1 Problem: There's been a *flood*.
   Advice: People should travel *by bus*.
2 Problem: There's a ....
   Advice: People shouldn't ....
3 Problem: There's a ....
   Advice: People should ....
4 Problem: There's an .... in the area.
   Advice: People must ....

Writing • Giving instructions

1 Read the travel advice quickly. Match the headings (a–e) to the blanks (1–3). There are two headings you don't need.

a After your trip   d What to pack
b Common problems   e During your trip
c How to prepare   *1*

Advice for travelers: **Climbing Mount Kilimanjaro**
(the highest mountain in Africa)

1 *How to prepare*
- You don't have to "climb" Kilimanjaro—you can walk all the way up! But it's a long walk, so you have to be in good shape. You should do a lot of walking before you come.
- You must see your doctor for vaccinations against diseases.
- You must book a trip with a group. You can't climb the mountain alone.

2 ....
- You must bring strong hiking boots.
- You should pack clothes for hot weather and cold weather.
- You must bring a lot of water so that you don't run out!

3 ....
- You shouldn't leave your climbing group. It's dangerous!
- You should walk slowly and take rests. Climbing too quickly might make you feel sick.
- Don't forget to have fun and take photos of all the amazing things you come across!

2 How many bullet points (•) does the writer include in the information pamphlet?

....

3 Think of an adventurous trip that people take in your country. Choose one of the ideas below, or use your own idea.

walking/biking in the mountains/desert/forest
kayaking/sailing/surfing on a river/in the ocean
(Where?)
Your idea: ....

4 You are going to write an information pamphlet like the one in Exercise 1. Complete the table with your ideas.

Advice for travelers: ....
(write your adventurous trip idea)

Heading 1: How to prepare
Do travelers need any special skills? Do they need to do any training/research/ other preparation?
• ....
• ....
• ....
Heading 2: ....
What kind of clothes/other equipment do travelers need?
• ....
• ....
• ....
Heading 3: ....
Are there any dangers? What other problems might people have? Any other tips?
• ....
• ....
• ....

5 Now write your information pamphlet using the title in Exercise 4. Use the ideas and paragraph plan in Exercises 1–4 and include a variety of modal verbs.

....
....
....
....
....
....
....
....
....
....
....
....
....
....
....
....
....
....

Check 2

Grammar

1 Choose the correct options.

New Message

Hello from New Zealand,
I ⁰ *can't* believe how beautiful the North Island is! You ¹....
definitely come here sometime—I think you'd love it.
Yesterday we explored the Tongariro National Park, where parts of
the *Lord of the Rings* movies ².... a few years ago. Apparently, this
area ³.... by thousands of Tolkien fans every year.
Today we ⁴.... kayaking on Lake Taupo! The trip ⁵.... at 11 a.m.,
but we ⁶.... arrive at 10 for a mandatory lesson. I hope I ⁷.... wet!
I better go now, or I ⁸.... behind. Wish me luck—I ⁹.... need it! ☺
Danny

Send

0 (a) can't	b shouldn't	c mustn't
1 a might	b should	c will
2 a made	b are made	c were made
3 a is visited	b visits	c will visit
4 a should go	b 're going	c go
5 a might start	b starts	c is started
6 a mustn't	b could	c have to
7 a can't get	b won't get	c aren't getting
8 a 'll leave	b 'm leaving	c 'll be left
9 a might	b must	c should

/ 9 points

2 Mark the correct sentences (✓) and rewrite the incorrect ones.

0 The cottage will be repaired by local builders. ✓
1 I work at the hotel next summer.
....
2 I can swim when I was only four.
....
3 Watch out! You'll hit that tree!
....
4 When invented ice cream?
....
5 The next train leaves at 12:35.
....

/ 5 points

Vocabulary

3 Choose the correct options.

0 Jess is an excellent team
communicator / (*player*) */
worker.*
1 We had dessert at the
ice cream *stood / stand /
standing.*
2 You should *make / do / take*
an appointment to see the
doctor.
3 I came *down / over / across*
a huge spider on the path.
4 Your work isn't *accurate /
experienced / patient.* It's full
of mistakes.
5 Let's sit under the beach
stand / umbrella / deck
for a while.
6 I can't figure *for / on / out*
the answer to this question.

/ 6 points

4 Complete the words in bold. Write *dis-* or *re-*.

A Help! I was ⁰ *re***searching**
information for my science
project when something
went wrong! All my files
have ¹.......**appeared**.
B OK, keep calm! I'll see if
I can ².......**store** them.
There ... I think I've
³ ....**covered** the files.
A Thank you, you're amazing!
I really ⁴.......**like** computers
sometimes ...
B I ⁵.......**agree** with you. I think
they make our lives easier!

/ 5 points

5 Complete the descriptions of three vacation photos.

Luxury Hotel in Singapore

Our hotel in Singapore was very beautiful. This is just the ⁰ front ¹d.......................... !

Summer in Italy

This is a photo of a brave ²s..........................standing next to mom's ³b.......................... ! I think it wanted our sandwiches.

Costa Rican Adventure

This is Mount Arenal, a ⁴v.......................... . We saw it ⁵e..........................with smoke, rocks and fire!

/ 5 points

Speaking

6 Choose the correct options.

A Hello. Langston College.

B Oh, hello. I'm ⁰ *asking / calling / ringing* about Jed Kane's photography class. I ¹ *would / like / 'd like* to enroll, please.

A I'm afraid it won't be possible to attend a class with Jed.

B Sorry, I don't ² *know / understand / see*. Are you ³ *saying / speaking / telling* that the course is canceled?

A No, but Mel Wyatt now teaches the class instead. The next class is tonight, in the Main Hall.

B Oh, I ⁴ *see / look / watch*! Could I enroll in Mel's class, please? And could you tell me how I ⁵ *direct / get / go* to the Main Hall from Green Street?

A Turn left and go ⁶ *along / pass / past* the library. ⁷ *Go / Take / Turn* the second turn on the right. The college is ⁸ *at / by / on* the left.

B Thanks!

A I'll just ⁹ *pass / give / transfer* you to our Education Officer. She'll take your information. ¹⁰ *Give / Hold / Wait* on please …

/ 10 points

Translation

7 Translate the sentences.

1 The house was buried by the avalanche.

....

2 I'm going to write a report about the harbor.

....

3 We must keep on walking, or we might not survive.

....

4 The old ice cream stand will be restored next year.

....

5 Many animals couldn't swim, so they drowned in the flood.

....

/ 5 points

Dictation

8 Listen and write.

21
1 ....
2 ....
3 ....
4 ....
5 ....

/ 5 points

Grammar Reference

Past simple vs Past continuous

Past simple
I played tennis.
We didn't (did not) play tennis.
Did you play tennis?   Yes, we did./No, we didn't.

Past continuous
I was playing tennis at two o'clock.
We weren't (were not) playing tennis at two o'clock.
Were you playing tennis at two o'clock?
Yes, we were./No, we weren't.

Past simple and Past continuous
When she arrived, he was playing tennis.
While he was playing tennis, she arrived.

Irregular verbs have different Past simple forms.
(See the **Irregular Verb List**, Workbook page 128.)

Use

- We use the Past simple for actions that began and finished in the past.
  *I **did** my homework last night.*

- We use the Past continuous for actions that were in progress at a certain time in the past.
  *I **was doing** my homework at eight o'clock last night.*

Stative verbs

We rarely use stative verbs in the continuous form. The most common stative verbs are the following:

- verbs to express thoughts and opinions: *believe, know, understand, remember, forget, think (= believe)*

- verbs to express likes, preferences, needs or wants: *like, love, prefer, hate, need, want*

- verbs to express state or possession: *be, have*
  *We **think** it's a good idea.   I **love** cats.*

When and while

- We use the Past simple and the Past continuous to describe two actions happening at the same time. We use the Past simple for the shorter action, and the Past continuous for the longer action in progress.

- To connect a Past simple and a Past continuous action, we often use *when* + Past simple or *while* + Past continuous.

*We were talking **when** the teacher **arrived**.*
*The teacher **arrived** **while** we **were talking**.*

- When we start a sentence with *when* or *while*, we use a comma.
  *When the teacher **arrived**, we **were talking**.*

Used to

Affirmative		
I/He/She/It We/You/They	used to like	cartoons.

Negative		
I/He/She/It We/You/They	didn't (did not) use to like	school.

Questions and short answers
Did I/he/she/it/we/you/they use to like candy?
Yes, I/he/she/it/we/you/they did.
No, I/he/she/it/we/you/they didn't.

Wh questions
What games did you use to play when you were little?

Use

- We use *used to* for past habits or situations that no longer exist in the present.
  *I **used to read** comics (but now I don't).*
  *We **didn't use to** drink coffee (but now we do).*

- We can use *used to* OR the Past simple to talk about past habits or situations.
  *She **used to walk** to school every day.*
  OR *She **walked** to school every day.*

- We do not use *used to* to talk about single, completed past actions. We use the Past simple instead.
  *I **watched** TV last night.*
  NOT ~~I used to watch TV last night.~~

Form

- In affirmative sentences, we use *used to* + infinitive.
  *We **used to swim** here.*

- In negative sentences and questions, we use *use to* (NOT ~~used to~~) + infinitive. We use an auxiliary verb (*did/didn't*).
  *I **didn't use to eat** vegetables.*
  *Did he **use to live** here?*

Grammar practice • Past simple vs Past continuous

1 Choose the correct verb forms.

1 When the teacher (came) / was coming in, everyone was talking.
2 This time last week I lay / was lying on the beach.
3 My mom met my dad while she travel / was traveling in the US.
4 I'm sorry, I didn't finish / wasn't finishing my homework yesterday.
5 He broke / was breaking his leg while he was playing soccer.
6 We didn't look / weren't looking at the camera when she took the photo.

2 Complete the conversation with the Past simple or Past continuous form of the verbs.

Mom ¹ Did you do (you/do) a lot of studying at the library this afternoon, Jake?

Jake Um, yes. I ² .... (study) really hard all afternoon!

Mom Really? What ³ .... (you/do) at four o'clock? I ⁴ .... (not see) you in the library, so you ⁵ .... (not study) right then.

Jake Oh, uh … Erin saw me while she ⁶ .... (walk) by. We ⁷ .... (take) a break for coffee. But while we ⁸ .... (sit) in the café, we tested each other on English grammar. Ask Erin if you don't believe me!

3 Write sentences or questions. Use the Past simple or Past continuous form of the verbs.

1 Last year / I / win / a scholarship
Last year I won a scholarship.
2 At eight o'clock last night / we / play / computer games
....
3 They / not live / here / three years ago
....
4 I / not sleep / when / you / call
....
5 She / not work / when / I / see / her
....
6 You / ask him his name / while / you / dance / ?
....

• Used to

4 Write sentences with used to and didn't use to to talk about what life was like 200 years ago.

1 people / drive cars
People didn't use to drive cars.
2 many American children / work
....
3 people / live as long
....
4 cities / be smaller
....
5 teenagers / wear jeans
....
6 people / not have / electricity at home
....

5 Complete the sentences and questions with the correct form of used to and the verb.

1 We didn't use to see (not see) each other very often.
2 **A** Where .... (you/go) on vacation when you were younger?
   B We .... (visit) my grandparents in Portland.
3 I .... (not like) going swimming.
4 **A** .... (they/play) basketball with you?
   B No, they ....
5 **A** .... (she/sit) next to you in class?
   B Yes, she ....

6 Rewrite the sentences and questions with the correct form of used to.

1 I loved playing card games.
I used to love playing card games.
2 My sister didn't drink much coffee.
....
3 How often did he call you?
....
4 Our neighbors had a noisy dog.
....
5 **A** Did your dad work here?
   B No, he didn't.
   .... ?
   ....

Grammar Reference

• Present perfect

Present perfect + *ever, never, already, yet*
The team's success on the soccer field has been huge.
Have you ever played soccer?
We watch soccer on TV, but we have never played it.
You've already formed a soccer team, but you haven't found a field yet!

Irregular verbs have different past participle forms. (See the **Irregular Verb List**, Workbook page 128.)

Use

We use the Present perfect to talk about:

* states, actions or events that started in the past and continue in the present.
  How long **have** *you* **known** *her?*

* past experiences, without saying exactly when they happened.
  I've **been** *to many different countries.*

* past events or situations with a result in the present.
  I've **lost** *my notebook, so I can't do my homework!*

Ever and *never*

* We use *ever* and *never* (= not ever) to refer to any time up to now.

* We use *ever/never* before the past participle.
  Have you **ever** *been to Canada?*
  I've **never** *written a novel.*

Already and *yet*

* We use *already* in affirmative sentences to emphasize that an action has happened.
  You've **already** *made a difference in people's lives.*

* We use *already* and *yet* before the past participle.

* We use *yet* in negative sentences to talk about an action that has not been completed, but that the speaker hopes will be completed in the future.
  I haven't seen the photo **yet***. I'd like to see it soon!*

* We use *yet* in questions to ask if an action has been completed.
  Have you finished your homework **yet***?*

* We use *yet* at the end of negative sentences and questions.

Present perfect with *since* and *for*

Since 2008, John has visited six countries.
I have now worked at the supermarket for two years.

Use

* We use *for* and *since* to answer the question *How long?*
  How long have you been here? I've been here for five days/since Sunday.

* We use *for* to refer to a period of time.
  For example: **for** *hours/two days/a month/a year/ my whole life/a while/ever.*
  I've worked here **for two weeks***.*
  He's been away **for a long time***.*

* We use *since* to talk about a point in time.
  For example: **since** *lunch/yesterday/last week/May/ 2010/my birthday/I was young.*
  I've lived here **since April***.*
  She's kept in touch **since she moved to Seattle***.*

• Present perfect vs Past simple

Present perfect
Nancy has written two novels.

Past simple
They practiced for hours every day.

Use

* We use the Present perfect to talk about a state or an action that happened in the past, but that has a result in the present or that continues in the present.

* We also use the Present perfect when we want to talk about a past event without saying exactly when it happened.
  He's already left. (It doesn't matter when he left.)
  I've lived here for two years. (I still live here now.)

* We use the Past simple to talk about a state or an action that finished in the past. We also use the Past simple to say exactly when something happened. We often use a time expression (e.g., *yesterday, last night*).
  I lived here in 1992.   He left last night.

Grammar practice • Present perfect + *ever*, *never*, *already*, *yet*, *since* and *for*

1 **Write questions with the Present perfect and *ever*. Answer them with the Present perfect and *never*.**

1 you / jump out / of a plane / ?
   Have you ever jumped out of a plane?
   No, *I've never jumped out of a plane.*
2 you / meet / the president of the United States / ?
   ....
   No, ...
3 your dad / win / a judo tournament / ?
   ....
   No, ...

2 **Write Present perfect sentences. Include the word in parentheses.**

1 my brother / arrive   (already)
   My brother's already arrived.
2 you / speak / to her / ?   (yet)
   ....
3 we / leave / school   (already)
   ....
4 I / eat / lunch   (already)
   ....
5 Ben / not hear / the song   (yet)
   ....
6 they / pay / you / ?   (yet)
   ....

3 **Complete the text. Use the Present perfect form of the verbs with *for* or *since*.**

I ¹ *'ve lived in this city since* (live/in this city) I was born. I ² .... (live/in this house) the last twelve years. My grandma ³ .... (live/in this house) her whole life. I ⁴ .... (have/my own room) I was eight. Obviously, it ⁵ .... (change/a lot) then. It used to have pink walls—yuck! The walls ⁶ .... (be/green) a long time—and they're now covered with posters.

4 **Complete the conversation with these time expressions.**

already	ever	for (x2)	never
since	~~yet~~	yet	

Faith Have you finished packing for our trip ¹ *yet*?
Jack No! I have tried to decide what to take ² .... days, but I only began packing about five minutes ago. I haven't gotten very far ³ ....
Faith Well, I've ⁴ .... packed my bag. I did it last night. So I could help you now if you like. I'm so excited! I've ⁵ .... been to Boston before. Have you ⁶ .... been there?
Jack A few times, but I haven't been there ⁷ .... years. In fact, I haven't been there ⁸ .... I was ten.

• Present perfect vs Past simple

5 **Choose the best options.**

1 **A** How many times (have you been) / did you go to Australia?
   B I *'ve never been / never went* to Australia.
2 I *'ve bought / bought* this bike last year.
3 *Have you told / Did you tell* her yet?
4 When I *'ve been / was* eight, I *'ve started / started* learning to play the piano.
5 We *haven't seen / didn't see* you for a while. How *have you been / were you*?
6 The city *has changed / changed* a lot since we first *have moved / moved* here.

6 **Complete the sentences. Use the Present perfect or the Past simple form of the verbs.**

1 *Did you hear* (you/hear) the storm last night?
2 This is the first time I .... (see) this movie.
3 She .... (travel) to many countries since she became famous.
4 Shakespeare .... (write) poems as well as plays.
5 I .... (never/see) a shark before!
6 They .... (make) it to the finals last week.

Grammar Reference

• Gerunds and infinitives

Use

Use the gerund (-*ing* form):	
after certain verbs	Please stop shouting!
after prepositions	I'm interested in studying emotions.
as the subject or object of a sentence	Smiling makes you happier.

Use the infinitive (with *to*):	
after certain verbs	I tried to smile.
after certain adjectives	It's wrong to lie.
to explain the purpose of an action	I called them to complain.

Form

We form the negative by putting *not* before the gerund or the infinitive.
*Imagine **not smiling** for a month!*
*I decided **not to go**.*

Verb + gerund

- These are some of the verbs that commonly take the gerund:

  advise   can't stand   consider   discuss
  dislike   enjoy   finish   hate   imagine
  keep   like   love   mention   (don't) mind
  miss   practice   prefer   recommend
  regret   stop   suggest

  *I **hate blushing**.*
  *He **can't stand screaming**.*

Verb + infinitive

- These are some of the verbs that commonly take the infinitive:

  afford   agree   appear   arrange   ask
  choose   decide   expect   hope   learn
  manage   mean   need   offer   plan
  pretend   promise   remember   refuse
  seem   try   wait   want

  *They **agreed to help**.*
  *I **decided to stay**.*

Adjective + infinitive

- These are some of the adjectives that commonly take the infinitive:

  difficult   easy   embarrassed   happy
  important   lucky   ready   right   sad
  stupid   surprised   wrong

  *I was **surprised to see** her.*
  *You were **lucky to survive**.*

• Present perfect continuous

Affirmative		
He/She/It I/You/We/They	's (has) been waiting 've (have) been waiting	for days.

Negative		
He/She/It I/You/We/They	hasn't (has not) been waiting haven't (have not) been waiting	for long.

Questions and short answers
Has he/she/it been waiting long?
Yes, he/she/it has.
No, he/she/it hasn't.
Have I/you/we/they been waiting long?
Yes, I/you/we/they have.
No, I/you/we/they haven't.

Wh questions
How long have you been waiting?

Use

We use the Present perfect continuous:

- to emphasize the length of an action that started in the past and that continues until the present.
  *I'm tired. **I've been working** hard all day.*
  *Where have you been? Jo**'s been looking** for you for hours!*

- to talk about an action that finished recently and that has a result in the present.
  *I'm sweating because **I've been running**.*
  *She's wet because she**'s been swimming**.*

We can use *for* and *since* with the Present perfect continuous.
*It's been raining **for days**.*
*We've been studying **since lunch**.*

Grammar practice • Gerunds and infinitives

1 **Complete the sentences with the gerund or infinitive form of the verb swim.**

1 It's good *to swim*.
2 I prefer ....
3 .... is my favorite sport.
4 I went to the pool ....
5 I tried ....
6 I'm not interested in ....

2 **Write the gerund or infinitive form of the verbs.**

1 We hope you enjoy *visiting* (visit) the sports hall of fame.
2 If you're interested in .... (find) out about the classes, please ask.
3 Please remember .... (follow) the rules.
4 .... (smoke) isn't allowed in the museum.
5 Please try .... (not/leave) anything behind.
6 Always buy a ticket! .... (not/pay) to enter the facilities is unlawful.

3 **Complete the text with the gerund or infinitive form of these verbs.**

| be | become | give | invent |
| make | perform | tell | |

[1] *Being* a professional comedian is a difficult job! It isn't easy [2] .... original ideas, and [3] .... in front of audiences can be scary. You have to work long hours if you want [4] .... successful, and you have to travel a lot [5] .... performances. But if you like [6] .... jokes, and you're good at [7] .... people laugh, it might be the job for you.

• Present perfect continuous

4 **Are these sentences correct (✓) or incorrect (✗)?**

1 He's been smiling all day.   ✓
2 I've been studied English since I was little.
3 My dog hasn't been eating well recently.
4 How long have they been living here?
5 Have you been working here long? No, I don't.
6 We've been knowing her for years.

5 **Complete the conversation with the Present perfect continuous form of the verbs.**

Tom You look tired.
Bella Yes, we [1] *'ve been working* (work) hard since lunch!
Kate I [2] .... (plant) vegetables in the rain! It [3] .... (rain) all day.
Bella I [4] .... (not help) in the yard, but I [5] .... (cook) in the kitchen for hours.
Kate What [6] .... (you/do) all day, Tom? [7] .... (you/work)?
Tom No, I [8] .... I [9] .... (relax)!

6 **Write sentences and questions. Use the Present perfect continuous form of the verbs in bold and add for or since.**

1 the children / **play** / three hours
  The children have been playing for three hours.
2 She / **cry** / she / read his text
  ....
3 We / **drive** / 8:30 this morning
  ....
4 you / **wait** / hours / ?
  ....
5 I / **not study** / Mandarin / very long
  ....
6 They / **not speak** / to each other / the argument
  ....
  ....

Grammar Reference

• Modal verbs: general points

Use

We use modal verbs before other verbs to add a special meaning to a sentence (for example, ability, advice).

Form

- We put an infinitive without *to* after most modal verbs:
  *We **must** go.   I **can hear** them.*

- We do not add an *-s* to modal verbs in the third person (with *he*, *she* or *it*).
  *He **can** stay.   It **should** stop.*

- We do not use *do/does* with modal verbs to form negatives, questions or short answers.
  *He **might not** come.*
  *Can I see her? No, you **can't**.*

- *Have to* is not a modal verb. We use *have to* differently:
  *She **has to** hurry.   I **don't have to** leave.*
  *Do I have to wait? Yes, you **do**.*

• Modals: ability, obligation, prohibition, advice

Ability
We can reduce the number of people who die.
We can't stop natural disasters.

Obligation
You must come to the school now.
They have to live on flat land near the ocean.
We don't have to lose huge numbers of lives.

Prohibition
You mustn't leave the shelter.

Advice
You should listen to the warnings.
You shouldn't go near the ocean.

Ability: *can, can't (cannot)*

- We use *can* or *can't* to talk about ability in the present.
  *He **can play** the guitar.*
  *I **can't see** you in the dark.*
  NOT *I don't see you in the dark.*

Obligation: *must, have to, don't have to*

- We use *must* or *have to* (which is not a modal verb) to talk about obligation in the present.
  *You **must do/have to do** your homework.*

- We use *don't have to* when there is NO obligation.
  *You **don't have to** come. It's your choice.*
  NOT *You mustn't come. It's your choice.*

Prohibition: *mustn't (must not)*

- We use *mustn't* to express a strong prohibition.
  *You **mustn't talk** here—it isn't allowed!*
  NOT *You don't have to talk here—it isn't allowed!*

Advice: *should, shouldn't (should not)*

- We use *should* to ask for and give advice.
  *What **should** I **do**? You **should call** for help.*

- We use *shouldn't* to say that we think something is a bad idea.
  *You **shouldn't swim** in that river—it's very deep.*

• Past modals

People could use schools as shelters.
I couldn't speak English when I was six.
They had to teach children about the dangers.
They didn't have to wait long for the next hurricane.

Ability in the past: *could, couldn't (could not)*

- We use *could* or *couldn't* to talk about ability in the past. We don't use *can* or *can't*.
  *She **could ski** when she was six.*
  NOT *She can ski when she was six.*
  *I **couldn't read** when I was two.*
  NOT *I can't read when I was two.*

Obligation in the past: *had to, didn't have to*

- We use *had to* or *didn't have to* to talk about obligation in the past.
  *She **had to wear** a uniform in elementary school.*
  *We **didn't have to go** to school last Monday.*

- We cannot use *must* for obligation in the past. We use *had to* instead.
  *She **must had to** wear a uniform in elementary school.*

Modals: possibility

That bite must hurt.

It might be a poisonous snake.

The bite could be really dangerous.

The snake can't be deadly.

Possibility: *could, might, might not*

- We use *could*, *might* and *might not* to suggest present or future possibility.
  You could be right—I'm not sure.
  The weather might be cold tomorrow. I don't know.
  He might not come. He hasn't decided yet.

Impossibility and certainty: *can't (cannot), must*

- We use *can't* when we think or guess that something is impossible.
  He can't be in Africa. I saw him in the mall today!
  Being an explorer can't be easy.

- We use *must* when we think or guess that something is certain.
  That man must feel scared. That snake looks terrifying!
  It must be late. It's getting dark.

Grammar practice • Modals: ability, obligation, prohibition, advice

1. Complete the text with these words.

~~can~~	can't	don't have to
must	mustn't	should

Anyone ¹ *can* learn surfing—but it takes a little time. You ² .... learn with a teacher—many people don't. However, if you want my advice, you ³ .... take at least one class. It's a really good idea!

Of course, you ⁴ .... be able to swim first. This is essential. If you ⁵ .... swim, you absolutely ⁶ .... try surfing—don't even think about it!

2. Rewrite the second sentence so that it has a similar meaning to the first.

1 I don't know how to ski.   (can)
  I can't ski.
2 It's a good idea to take bug spray.   (should)
  You ....
3 Don't swim here!   (must)
  You ....
4 Wearing safety glasses is optional.   (have to)
  You ....
5 He knows how to skate.   (can)
  He ....

Past modals

3. Put the modals into the past form.

1 She *could* (can) play the violin when she was six.
2 We ....(have to) work hard last year.
3 I .... (can) read when I was five.
4 You .... (don't have to) help her yesterday.
5 He .... (can't) do last night's science homework.

Modals: possibility

4. Choose the best option.

1 It might / must / can't be sunny tomorrow. I hope so!
2 It could / must / can't be her birthday. She had a birthday party last month!
3 You can't / could / must be right. I'm not sure.
4 Being in a tornado must / can't / could be terrifying—that's for certain.
5 I must / can't / might have some water in my bag. Hang on—I'll look.

5. Complete the sentences. Write *could, might, can't* or *must*.

1 He *could* be her brother. They look alike.
2 She .... be good at math. She got a high grade on her exam!
3 You .... be tired. We've only been walking for ten minutes!
4 She .... be at home. I'm not sure.
5 They .... be cold. They're shivering!

Vocabulary

Different Lives

Unit vocabulary

1 Translate the words.

Compound nouns

babysitter ....
businessperson ....
classmate ....
firefighter ....
homework ....
lighthouse ....
skyscraper ....
snowmobile ....
spaceship ....
speedboat ....
whiteboard ....
windmill ....

2 Translate the words.

Phrasal verbs 1

count on ....
fill out ....
find out ....
get back ....
give up ....
go out ....
hang out ....
look for ....
run away ....
set up ....

Vocabulary extension

3 Match the photos to the compound nouns in the box. Use your dictionary if necessary. Write the words in English and in your language.

| haircut | ~~headphones~~ | highway |
| playground | seatbelt | weightlifter |

1 ....*headphones*............
....

2 ....
....

3 ....
....

4 ....
....

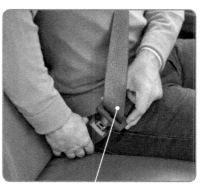

5 ....
....

6 ....
....

Vocabulary

Aiming High

Unit vocabulary

1 Translate the expressions.

Collocations with *make*, *go* and *keep*

go crazy ....

go for a walk ....

go together ....

go well ....

keep a secret ....

keep calm ....

keep control ....

keep in touch ....

make a decision ....

make a difference ....

make it to the finals ....

make someone's dream come true
....

2 Translate the words.

Jobs and suffixes *-or, -er, -ist*

art ....

artist ....

novel ....

novelist ....

photograph ....

photographer ....

play ....

playwright ....

poem ....

poet ....

sculptor ....

sculpture ....

Vocabulary extension

3 Match the photos to the collocations in the box. Use your dictionary if necessary. Write the expressions in English and in your language.

| go on vacation | ~~go shopping~~ | keep a diary |
| keep in shape | make a mistake | make friends |

1 .... *go shopping* ....

2 ....
....

3 ....
....

4 ....
....

5 ....
....

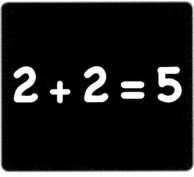

6 ....
....

Vocabulary

Be Happy!

Unit vocabulary

1 Translate the words.

Showing feelings

blush ....
cry ....
frown ....
gasp ....
laugh ....
scream ....
shiver ....
shout ....
sigh ....
smile ....
sweat ....
yawn ....

2 Translate the words.

Adjective suffixes

beautiful ....
dangerous ....
famous ....
healthy ....
lucky ....
peaceful ....
poisonous ....
successful ....
wealthy ....

Vocabulary extension

3 Match the photos to the adjectives in the box. Use your dictionary if necessary. Write the words in English and in your language.

| annoyed | excited | jealous | proud | relaxed | ~~stressed~~ |

1 .... *stressed* ....
....

2 ....
....

3 ....
....

4 ....
....

5 ....
....

6 ....
....

Vocabulary

Survive!

Unit vocabulary

1 Translate the words.

Natural disasters

Nouns

avalanche ....

disease ....

drought ....

earthquake ....

famine ....

flood ....

hurricane ....

tsunami ....

volcano ....

Verbs

bury ....

destroy ....

drown ....

erupt ....

spread ....

starve ....

survive ....

2 Translate the phrasal verbs.

Phrasal verbs 2

break down ....

calm down ....

come across ....

figure out ....

get through ....

keep on ....

look forward to ....

put on ....

run out of ....

take off ....

Vocabulary extension

3 Match the pictures to the verbs in the box. Use your dictionary if necessary. Write the words in English and in your language.

| burn | crash | freeze | injure | rescue | ~~sink~~ |

1 ....*sink*............

....

2 ....

....

3 ....

....

4 ....

....

5 ....

....

6 ....

....

Speaking and Listening

Expressing extremes

● Speaking

(1) **Choose the correct options. Then listen and check.**

32
1 **A** I'm *so* / *such* tired! I've had *so* / *such* a hard day.
  B Well, sit down, and I'll make you a cup of coffee.
2 **A** Max has really changed, hasn't he?
  B Definitely! He used to be *such* / *really* shy. Now he's *such* / *so* friendly.
3 **A** How was your vacation?
  B Great! We had *so* / *such* a good time. New Orleans is *really* / *such* beautiful.

(2) **Complete the conversation with these phrases.**
33 **Then listen and check.**

really easy	really hungry	so difficult
so good	~~so sad~~	such a bad
such a good		

Scott What's up, Paula? Why do you look ¹ *so sad*?

Paula Hi, Scott. I'm having ² .... day. I just had my first driving lesson. I was terrible! It was ³ ....

Scott Don't worry! After a few weeks, it'll seem ⁴ .... You'll be fine!

Paula Thanks, Scott. You're ⁵ .... friend. You always say the right thing!

Scott Let's go to Rosa's Café. I'm ⁶ .... , and the pastries at Rosa's are ⁷ .... you'll feel better soon.

● Listening

(3) **Listen to the conversation. Match the people**
34 **(1–5) to the names (a–e).**

1 uncle
2 friend
3 sister
4 grandmother
5 niece

a Angela
b Lottie Field
c Ellis
d Kayla
e Charlotte West

(4) **Listen again. Complete the sentences. Write one**
34 **or two words in each blank.**

1 Ellis says the news makes him feel *really old*.
2 Angela thinks the baby has such .... name.
3 Ellis's sister named the baby after ....
4 The picture on Ellis's phone isn't very good because the baby was ....
5 Angela thinks that Ellis and the baby have similar ....
6 Ellis doesn't want to be .... until the baby is older.

Speaking and Listening

Giving/Responding to news

• Speaking

1 Choose the correct options to complete
35 the conversation. Then listen and check.

Arthur What's ¹ *on* / *up*, Jess?

Jess I ² *just* / *now* heard some amazing news! You won't ³ *believe* / *think* it, but we've made it to the finals of the dance competition!

Arthur ⁴ *Not* / *No* way!

Jess ⁵ *Serious* / *Seriously*.

Arthur But I thought everyone hated us! ⁶ *What* / *How* happened?

Jess Well, we were wrong! They loved us!

Arthur ⁷ *Believable!* / *Unbelievable!*

Jess And I have even more good news … we've won a $50 prize!

Arthur You ⁸ *kid* / *'re kidding* me! Wow.

2 Complete the conversations. Write one word
36 in each blank. Then listen and check.

1 **A** What's *up*, Josh? Are you OK?
   B I'm OK, thanks. But I .... heard some sad news.

2 **A** I got 100% on my exam!
   B No .... ! You're kidding me.
   A Seriously. I swear it's ....

3 **A** You .... believe it, but I just heard about something amazing.
   B .... happened?

• Listening

3 Listen to the conversation. What's the main
37 piece of news for Barney and Scarlett?

a They aren't going on vacation this year. ☐
b They're now millionaire lottery winners. ☐
c They're going on an exciting vacation. ☐

4 Listen again. Choose the best options.
37
1 *Dad* / *Barney* called *Dad* / *Barney*.
2 Scarlett is reading a *book* / *magazine*.
3 Last summer, Barney and Scarlett went to *Las Vegas* / *Paris* / *New York City*.
4 This year, Barney and Scarlett are going to *Las Vegas* / *Paris* / *New York City*.
5 Dad has already paid for the *hotel rooms* / *plane tickets*.
6 Dad *won* / *didn't win* a lottery prize.

Speaking and Listening

Invitations

• Speaking

(1) Put the words in the correct order. Then listen
38 and check.

1 **A** *Do you want to meet us at the café?*
  meet / you / us / want / Do / at the café /
  to / ?
  B OK, thanks. ....
  you / I'll / there / see
2 **A** ....
  shopping / feel / going / like / Do / you / ?
  B Sorry. ....
  say / I / no / have to
3 **A** ....
  you / play / Would / basketball / like / to / ?
  B ....
  fun, / That / I'm sorry, / sounds / I / like /
  can't / but

(2) Complete the conversation with these words and
39 phrases. Then listen and check.

~~feel like~~	great	I'd	I'll
'm sorry	like	Sorry	want

Nell Do you ¹ *feel like* going for a bike ride
       tomorrow?
Tom That sounds like fun, but I can't.
       I ² .... I don't have a bike.
Nell Well, would you ³ ....
       to go swimming?
Tom ⁴ .... I have to say no.
       I hate swimming!
Nell OK. Do you ⁵ .... to play
       video games, as usual?
Tom That's a ⁶ .... idea.
       ⁷ .... love to. But let's meet
       at my house. Come over at 12, and I'll
       make you lunch.
Nell OK, thanks. ⁸ ....
       see you there!

• Listening

(3) Listen to the phone conversations. Answer
40 the questions. Use names from the box.

Alice	Bethany	Dan	Mark	Tessa

1 Who does Mark phone?
  Bethany, Dan and Alice
2 Who really likes Tessa?
  ....
3 Who's tired?
  ....
4 Who's visiting grandparents?
  ....
5 Who's going on the picnic?
  .... , ... ,
  .... , and ....

(4) Listen again. Complete the information about
40 the picnic.

1 Day: *Saturday*
2 Place: ....
3 Time: ....
4 Food: .... , ...
  and ....
5 Drinks: .... and ....

Speaking and Listening

Asking for clarification

• Speaking

1 **Choose the correct options. Then listen and check.**
41

Nina You ¹*should don't wear /*
shouldn't wear that T-shirt!

Stella What ²*do you mean /*
are you meaning? ³*Do you*
say / Are you saying that you
don't like this T-shirt?

Nina No, but it's the wrong color
for walking in the desert.

Stella Sorry, I ⁴*don't understand /*
haven't been understanding.
Why is it wrong?

Nina Well, black keeps you warm.
You should wear white or a
light color to stay cool.

Stella Oh, ⁵*I've seen / I see*! Thanks.
I'll find another one …

2 **Complete the conversation. Write**
42 **one word in each blank. Then listen**
and check.

Lara You ¹*should* take sunscreen
and sunglasses if you're
walking in the Rocky
Mountains in winter.

Owen Sorry, I ²........................
understand. Are you
³........................ that the
Rocky Mountains will be *hot*
in January?

Lara No, but you'll need
sunscreen!

Owen What ⁴........................
⁵........................ mean?

Lara Well, the sun on the snow is
very bright. Your skin might
burn.

Owen ⁶........................ , I see!
Thanks.

• Listening

3 **Listen to the conversation and answer the questions.**
43
1 Why does Lucy want to stop? Choose *two* reasons.
She's …
a tired. ☐ **b** cold. ☐ **c** hungry. ☐
2 Which places do Bart and Lucy visit? Choose *two*.
a a river ☐ **b** a field ☐ **c** the woods ☐
3 What problems do Bart and Lucy have? Choose *two*.

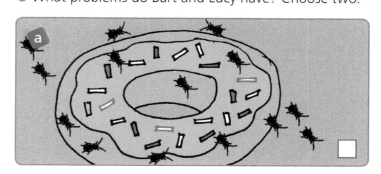

4 **Listen again and complete the sentences.**
43
1 Lucy wants to stop *walking*.
2 Lucy thinks that the .... are very pretty.
3 Lucy and Bart reach the field .... minutes later.
4 .... sees the café first.
5 .... doesn't think they should go into the café.
6 .... thinks the café will be a nice place to eat
because it doesn't have ....

Pronunciation

Consonants

Symbol	Example	Your examples
/p/	pen	
/b/	book	
/t/	tea	
/d/	desk	
/k/	cat	
/g/	girl	
/tʃ/	cheese	
/dʒ/	June	
/f/	five	
/v/	very	
/θ/	thin	
/ð/	then	
/s/	so	
/z/	zoo	
/ʃ/	she	
/ʒ/	usually	
/h/	hat	
/m/	man	
/n/	now	
/ŋ/	thing	
/l/	long	
/r/	red	
/y/	yes	
/w/	week	

Vowels

Symbol	Example	Your examples
/ɪ/	sit	
/ɛ/	ten	
/æ/	black	
/ɑ/	hot	
/ʌ/	up	
/ʊ/	full	
/i/	see	
/eɪ/	pay	
/aɪ/	why	
/ɔɪ/	enjoy	
/u/	too	
/oʊ/	home	
/aʊ/	loud	
/ɪr/	year	
/ɛr/	wear	
/ɑr/	far	
/ɔ/	dog	
/ʊr/	sure	
/ɔr/	door	
/ə/	ago	
/ɚ/	shirt	

Pronunciation practice

Unit 1 • Compound noun word stress

1 Listen and repeat. Then mark the main stress
59 in each word. Answer the question below.

1 classmate   4 spaceship
2 lighthouse   5 snowmobile
3 skyscraper   6 windmill

Do we usually stress the *first*, *second* or *last*
syllable in compound nouns? ....

2 Mark the main stress. Then listen, check
60 your answers and repeat.

1 bedroom   4 hairstylist
2 whiteboard   5 supermarket
3 notebook   6 newspaper

Unit 2 • Sentence stress

1 Listen and repeat. Then mark the stressed words.
61
1 We're happy because we made it to the finals.
2 Can you help me? Do these clothes
   go together?
3 You've made our dreams come true.

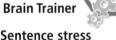

> **Brain Trainer**
>
> **Sentence stress**
> We usually stress the most important content words in
> sentences (often main verbs, nouns and adjectives).
>
> **Now do Exercise 2.**

2 Mark the *three* most important content words in
62 each sentence. Then listen, check your answers
and repeat the sentences, copying the stress.

1 I've made a very big decision.
2 My sister has moved to Alaska.
3 We went for a walk in the park.
4 Have you heard the news? I'm so excited!

Unit 3 • Showing feelings

1 Listen. You will hear a speaker say "Did you
63 see that?" in four different conversations.
Is the speaker *afraid*, *angry*, *bored* or *excited*?

1 ....   3 ....
2 ....   4 ....

2 Read the sentences. Do you think the speakers will
64 sound *afraid*, *angry*, *bored* or *excited*? Listen, check
your answers and repeat, copying the intonation.

1 I won the lottery!
2 There's nothing to do here.
3 What's that noise?
4 Never lie to me again!

Unit 4 • Consonant clusters

1 Listen and repeat. Do the <u>underlined</u> letters
65 have *one*, *two* or *three* consonant sounds?

a <u>squ</u>are   he<u>lps</u>   e<u>xp</u>ensive
b wea<u>th</u>er   <u>wh</u>ite   si<u>ck</u>
c bui<u>ld</u>ing   ti<u>met</u>able   fini<u>sh</u>ed

2 <u>Underline</u> the consonant clusters. Then listen
66 and repeat.

1 The bus stops on a quiet street.
2 I remember her wonderful home in the country.
3 He found her passport in the suitcase.

Unit 5 • /ɚ/ and /ɔr/

1 Listen and repeat. Then <u>underline</u> the sounds
67 /ɚ/ or /ɔr/.

/ɚ/   learn   third   dessert
/ɔr/   warm   before   north

2 Complete the table. Then listen, check and repeat.
68

<u>affo</u>rd	<u>bo</u>red	<u>ea</u>rly	<u>floo</u>r	<u>jou</u>rney	<u>wo</u>rld

/ɚ/	/ɔr/
....	....
....	....
....	....

Irregular Verb List

Verb	Past Simple	Past Participle
be	was/were	been
become	became	become
begin	began	begun
break	broke	broken
bring	brought	brought
build	built	built
buy	bought	bought
can	could	been able
catch	caught	caught
choose	chose	chosen
come	came	come
cost	cost	cost
cut	cut	cut
do	did	done
draw	drew	drawn
drink	drank	drunk
drive	drove	driven
eat	ate	eaten
fall	fell	fallen
feed	fed	fed
feel	felt	felt
fight	fought	fought
find	found	found
fly	flew	flown
forget	forgot	forgotten
get	got	gotten
give	gave	given
go	went	gone/been
have	had	had
hear	heard	heard
hold	held	held
keep	kept	kept
know	knew	known
leave	left	left
lend	lent	lent

Verb	Past Simple	Past Participle
light	lit	lit
lose	lost	lost
make	made	made
mean	meant	meant
meet	met	met
pay	paid	paid
put	put	put
read /rid/	read /rɛd/	read /rɛd/
ride	rode	ridden
ring	rang	rung
run	ran	run
say	said	said
see	saw	seen
sell	sold	sold
send	sent	sent
shine	shone	shone
show	showed	shown
sing	sang	sung
sit	sat	sat
sleep	slept	slept
speak	spoke	spoken
spend	spent	spent
stand	stood	stood
steal	stole	stolen
swim	swam	swum
take	took	taken
teach	taught	taught
tell	told	told
think	thought	thought
throw	threw	thrown
understand	understood	understood
wake	woke	woken
wear	wore	worn
win	won	won
write	wrote	written

My Assessment Profile Starter Unit

1. What can I do? Mark (✓) the options in the table.

⏪ = I need to study this again. ⏸ = I'm not sure about this. ▶ = I'm happy with this. ⏩ = I do this very well.

		⏪	⏸	▶	⏩
Grammar (pages 4–7)	• I can use all forms of *be* and *have* in the Present simple. • I can use all forms of the Present simple and Present continuous, and I understand when to use each tense. • I can use apostrophes, pronouns and possessive adjectives correctly. • I can make comparisons using comparative and superlative adjectives, and *too* and *enough*. • I can use relative pronouns in defining relative clauses. • I can talk about quantity using *some*, *any*, *much*, *many* and *a lot of*. • I can use regular and irregular forms of the Past simple.				
Vocabulary (pages 4–7)	• I can talk about daily routines, free-time activities and feelings. • I can use different adjectives correctly. • I can tell the time.				
Listening (page 8)	• I can understand a conversation between friends.				
Speaking (page 8)	• I can ask for and give information about other people.				
Reading (page 9)	• I can understand an informal email giving news.				
Writing (page 9)	• I can write a description of a friend.				

2. What new words and expressions can I remember?

words ....

expressions ....

3. How can I practice other new words and expressions?

record them on my MP3 player ☐   write them in a notebook ☐
practice them with a friend ☐   translate them into my language ☐

4. What English have I learned outside class?

	words	expressions
on the radio		
in songs		
in movies		
on the Internet		
on TV		
with friends		

My Assessment Profile   Unit

1 What can I do? Mark (✓) the options in the table.

⏪ = I need to study this again.   ⏸ = I'm not sure about this.   ▶ = I'm happy with this.   ⏩ = I do this very well.

		⏪	⏸	▶	⏩
Vocabulary (pages 10 and 13)	• I can form and use compound nouns to talk about jobs, transportation, school and buildings. • I can understand and use ten phrasal verbs.				
Pronunciation (page 10)	• I can use the correct stress in compound nouns.				
Reading (pages 11 and 16)	• I can read and understand an article about different people's daily lives, and an article about a man with an unusual job.				
Grammar (pages 12 and 15)	• I can understand when to use the Past simple or the Past continuous. • I can use the Past simple and the Past continuous in sentences with *when* and *while*. • I can use all forms of *used to* to talk about past habits.				
Speaking (page 14)	• I can express extremes using *so*, *such* and *really*.				
Listening (pages 14 and 16)	• I can understand a conversation between friends and a radio show.				
Writing (page 17)	• I can use a variety of past tenses correctly. • I can write a short story.				

2 What new words and expressions can I remember?

words ....

expressions ....

3 How can I practice other new words and expressions?

record them on my MP3 player ☐   write them in a notebook ☐

practice them with a friend ☐   translate them into my language ☐

4 What English have I learned outside class?

	words	expressions
on the radio		
in songs		
in movies		
on the Internet		
on TV		
with friends		

My Assessment Profile Unit

1. What can I do? Mark (✓) the options in the table.

⏪ = I need to study this again.　⏸ = I'm not sure about this.　▶ = I'm happy with this.　⏩ = I do this very well.

		⏪	⏸	▶	⏩
Vocabulary (pages 20 and 23)	• I can understand and use twelve collocations with *make*, *go* and *keep*. • I can form words for talking about jobs with *-er, -or, -ist* and other suffixes.				
Pronunciation (page 20)	• I can use the correct stress in sentences.				
Reading (pages 21 and 26)	• I can read and understand an article about an unusual soccer team, and an article about two very successful people.				
Grammar (pages 22 and 25)	• I can use the Present perfect with *ever, never, already* and *yet* correctly. • I can use the Present perfect with *for* and *since* correctly. • I can understand when to use the Present perfect or the Past simple.				
Speaking (page 24)	• I can give and respond to news.				
Listening (pages 24 and 26)	• I can understand a conversation between friends and a news show.				
Writing (page 27)	• I can use different time expressions. • I can write a biography.				

2. What new words and expressions can I remember?

words ....

expressions ....

3. How can I practice other new words and expressions?

record them on my MP3 player ☐　　write them in a notebook ☐

practice them with a friend ☐　　translate them into my language ☐

4. What English have I learned outside class?

	words	expressions
on the radio		
in songs		
in movies		
on the Internet		
on TV		
with friends		

My Assessment Profile Unit  3

1 **What can I do? Mark (✓) the options in the table.**

⏮ = I need to study this again. ⏸ = I'm not sure about this. ▶ = I'm happy with this. ⏭ = I do this very well.

		⏮	⏸	▶	⏭
Vocabulary (pages 30 and 33)	• I can talk about feelings and the way we express them. • I can form adjectives from nouns using the suffixes -*ful*, -*ous* and -*y*.				
Pronunciation (page 30)	• I can use intonation to express anger, boredom, excitement and fear.				
Reading (pages 31 and 36)	• I can read and understand an article about smiling, and an article about two different views of fame.				
Grammar (pages 32 and 35)	• I can use gerunds after certain verbs and prepositions, and as the subject or object of a sentence. • I can use infinitives after certain verbs and adjectives, and to express purpose. • I can use the Present perfect continuous to talk about longer actions that started in the past and continue until the present.				
Speaking (pages 34 and 35)	• I can make and respond to invitations.				
Listening (pages 34–36)	• I can understand a conversation between friends and a radio interview.				
Writing (page 37)	• I can add and contrast ideas using linking words. • I can write a "for and against" essay.				

2 **What new words and expressions can I remember?**

words ....

expressions ....

3 **How can I practice other new words and expressions?**

record them on my MP3 player ☐   write them in a notebook ☐

practice them with a friend ☐   translate them into my language ☐

4 **What English have I learned outside class?**

	words	expressions
on the radio		
in songs		
in movies		
on the Internet		
on TV		
with friends		

My Assessment Profile   Unit

1 **What can I do? Mark (✓) the options in the table.**

⏪ = I need to study this again.   ⏸ = I'm not sure about this.   ▶ = I'm happy with this.   ⏩ = I do this very well.

		⏪	⏸	▶	⏩
Vocabulary (pages 44 and 47)	• I can use nouns and verbs to talk about natural disasters. • I can understand and use ten phrasal verbs.				
Pronunciation (page 44)	• I can pronounce consonant clusters correctly.				
Reading (pages 45 and 50)	• I can read and understand an article about cyclones in Bangladesh and an article about a survival story.				
Grammar (pages 46, 47 and 49)	• I can use modals to talk about ability, obligation, prohibition and advice in the present. • I can use modals to talk about ability and obligation in the past. • I can use modals to talk about possibility and certainty in the present.				
Speaking (pages 48 and 49)	• I can ask for clarification.				
Listening (pages 48–50)	• I can understand a conversation between friends and someone giving advice.				
Writing (page 51)	• I can organize my writing clearly to give instructions. • I can write an information pamphlet.				

2 **What new words and expressions can I remember?**

words ....

expressions ....

3 **How can I practice other new words and expressions?**

record them on my MP3 player ☐   write them in a notebook ☐
practice them with a friend ☐   translate them into my language ☐

4 **What English have I learned outside class?**

	words	expressions
on the radio		
in songs		
in movies		
on the Internet		
on TV		
with friends		

Notes

Notes

Notes

Notes

Pearson Education Limited
Edinburgh Gate
Harlow
Essex CM20 2JE
England
and Associated Companies throughout the world.

www.pearsonelt.com/moveit

© Pearson Education Limited 2015

The right of Katherine Stannett, Fiona Beddall and Bess Bradfield to be identified as the authors of this work has been asserted by them in accordance with the Copyright, Designs and Patents Act, 1988.

All rights reserved. No part of this publication may be reproduced, stored in a retrieval system, or transmitted in any form or by any means, electronic, mechanical, photocopying, recording, or otherwise without the prior written permission of the Publishers.

First published 2015
Fifth impression 2019

Set in 10.5/12.5pt LTC Helvetica Neue Light
ISBN: 978-1-2921-0137-8

Printed by CPI Group (UK) Ltd, Croydon CR0 4YY

Acknowledgements

We are grateful to the following for permission to reproduce copyright material:
Article 1.3 adapted from www.hackneygazette.co.uk/news/bee_inspired_how_bee_keeping_changed_one_man's_life_1_101162, Hackney Gazette; Emma Bartholomew; September 2011

Photo Acknowledgements

The publisher would like to thank the following for their kind permission to reproduce their photographs:

(Key: b-bottom; c-centre; l-left; r-right; t-top)

Students' Book:
Alamy Images: 1exposure 39, AfriPics.com 44 (a), Russell Blake 36r, Neil Cooper 45br, Rod Haestier 44 (c), Grant Rooney 65br, Penny Tweedie 26tr, View Stock 66bc, David White 44 (f), whiteboxmedia limited 64br, Ed Zetera 47; **(c) Telegraph Media Group:** Kyoto Hmada 26tl; **Corbis:** Ashley Cooper 44 (e), Jim Edds 44 (g), Rob Howard 45l, Buddy Mays 11 (b), Minden Pictures / Pete Oxford 60/7, Ocean 11 (a), Tim Pannell 60/8, Keren Su 33r, David Turnley 44 (b); **Fotolia.com:** EpicStockMedia 60/3, Pavel Timofeev 60/2; **Getty Images:** AFP / Farjana K. Godhuly 45cr, Digital Vision / Natphotos 60/1, hemis.fr / Christophe Boisvieux 33bl, Imagemore Co, Ltd 11 (c); **iStockphoto:** oblachko 29tr, 53tr; **Leo Burnett Group Thailand:** Client: TMB Bank, Creative Agency: Leo Burnett Group Thailand, Production Company: Revolver, Director: The Glue Society 21tl, 21b; **Pearson Education Ltd:** Gareth Boden 8, 9, 14, 24, 34, 48; **Press Association Images:** PA Wire / Andrew Milligan 29l, 29r; **Rex Features:** James Fraser 60/5, Nils Jorgensen 62, Newspix 65bl, Sims / Beretta 60/4, Sipa Press 65tr, 66r; **Science Photo Library Ltd:** Peter Menzel 44 (h); **Shutterstock.com:** beboy 44 (i), danymages 16, darios 19tr, Kevin Eaves 60/6, Helga Esteb 27, iofoto 64tr, Monkey Business Images 64bl, StudioSmart 19 (background); **SuperStock:** age fotostock 53cr, Blend Images 36l, Blue Jean Images 66bl, Corbis 61, Image Source 60/9, moodboard 32, Rapsodia 44 (d); **Jason O. Watson Photography, LLC:** 50; **WildlifeDirect / Paula Kahumbu:** 53tl, 53br

Workbook:
Action Plus Sports Images: Stephen Bartholomew 118cr; **Alamy Images:** Hermes Images 77bl, Tomas Kraus 77tr, Adrian Muttitt 77br, Adrian Sherratt 77tl, Jack Sullivan 119bl; **Corbis:** Citizen Stock / Sherrie Nickol 71l, Macduff Everton 109bl, Hulton-Deutsch Collection 79, Inmagine Asia 120bl, Lauryn Ishak 109tl, Dirk Lindner 96tc, Ocean 120cl; **Fotolia.com:** 129-133; **Getty Images:** E+ / zorani 120cr; **Pearson Education Ltd:** Studio 8 122cr, Tudor Photography 122br; **Shutterstock.com:** chrisdorney 109cl, Alexander Demyanenko 118tl, Eder 78t, Elena Elisseeva 118bl, R. Gino Santa Maria 123b, Natali Glado 83, Andreas Gradin 96tr, Chaikovskiy Igor 78b, Iryna1 99, jjphotos 118tr, Dmitry Kalinovsky 90cr, Stanislav Komogorov 95, Aleksandr Markin 119tr, Tyler Olson 118cl, stocknadia 123t; **SuperStock:** Ableimages 120tl, age fotostock 90bl, 96tl, Belinda Images 120tr, Blend Images 76, 90tl, 90tr, 90br, 119cr, Cultura Limited 89, 105tr, Cusp 105tl, Image Source 120br, PhotoAlto 119cl, Pixtal 90cl, Tetra Images 118br, 119tl

Cover images: *Front:* **Corbis:** PhotoAlto / Laurence Mouton

All other images © Pearson Education

Every effort has been made to trace the copyright holders and we apologise in advance for any unintentional omissions. We would be pleased to insert the appropriate acknowledgement in any subsequent edition of this publication.

Special thanks to the following for their help during location photography: East Herts District Council; Harlow Town Council; Naze Tower www.naze-tower.co.uk; Tendring Council; Matthew Dickin; Jackie Dynamou; Anne and Ben Meaden; JoJo Notley

Illustrated by

Students' Book:
Peskimo; Paula Franco; Moreno Chiacchiera; Chris Coady; Matt Roussel.

Workbook:
Chris Coady; Julian Mosedale; Paula Franco; Peskimo.